This is believed to be the first book of its kind. Twelve distinguished actors were asked to write about the preparation and performance of a Shakespeare role they had played in a production with the Royal Shakespeare Company. The contributors are Patrick Stewart, Sinead Cusack, Donald Sinden, John Bowe, Geoffrey Hutchings, Brenda Bruce, Tony Church, Michael Pennington, Richard Pasco, Roger Rees, Gemma Jones and David Suchet. Each has concentrated on one character, sometimes played over a number of years in different productions, and each account is illustrated with photographs.

In editing the essays Philip Brockbank has been concerned to preserve the actors' individual voices. A note at the beginning of each essay identifies the relevant productions and the book opens with a brief perspective on the English acting tradition revealed in the material that follows.

It is a unique record. For those who remember the productions at Stratford-upon-Avon, London, or on tour, the actors reveal something of the technique and experience behind their performances. Taken together the essays have a more permanent significance, providing a many-angled account of the actor's professional discipline and the creative instability of his art. Shakespeare's characters are not fixed: each role develops and alters with each audience as the player struggles to create a fresh and convincing character from the often conflicting demands of Shakespeare's text, the director's conception, the theatrical and scholarly traditions, and his own individual instinct and personality.

The book will appeal to all theatregoers and lovers of Shakespeare, to actors, students and teachers and those seeking a better understanding of Shakespeare as an actor's playwright.

Players of Shakespeare

Players of Shakespeare

Essays in Shakespearean performance by
twelve players with the
Royal Shakespeare Company

Edited by Philip Brockbank
Director, The Shakespeare Institute
University of Birmingham, Stratford-upon-Avon

The right of the
University of Cambridge
to print and sell
all manner of books
was granted by
Henry VIII in 1534.
The University has printed
and published continuously
since 1584.

Cambridge University Press

Cambridge
London   New York   New Rochelle
Melbourne   Sydney

Published by the Press Syndicate of the University of Cambridge
The Pitt Building, Trumpington Street, Cambridge CB2 1RP
32 East 57th Street, New York, NY 10022, USA
10 Stamford Road, Oakleigh, Melbourne 3166, Australia

First published 1985
Reprinted 1986

Printed in Great Britain at
the University Press, Cambridge

Library of Congress catalogue card number: 84–28484

British Library cataloguing in publication data

Players of Shakespeare: Essays in Shakespearean
performance.
1. Shakespeare, William – Dramatic production
I. Brockbank, Philip
792.9   PR3091
ISBN 0 521 24428 5

Contents

Illustrations

We are grateful to the following for permission to reproduce photographs: Joe Cocks Studio for Figs. 1, 2, 3, 4, 5, 6b, 10, 12, 13, 14, 16, 17, 18, 22, 23, 24, 25, 26, 27, 28, 29; Donald Cooper for Figs. 20 and 21; Nobby Clark for Fig. 15; the *Stratford-upon-Avon Herald* for Fig. 19; and Reg Wilson for Fig. 11.

Foreword

Contributors were invited to write about roles that they had successfully realized in the theatre – and sometimes talked about in courses given at the Shakespeare Institute. They were asked not to provide a general account, whether historical or personal, of the play overall, or of the production itself, but to concentrate on the actor's work in creating a Shakespearean character on stage. The aim was not stage history of the traditional kind, nor theatrical reminiscence, but commentary illuminating the role and revealing the actor's professional disciplines. Some accounts have been written out of current experience of a production and some are retrospective.

There are no exact models for this collection, though there have been many published interviews with actors, both in periodicals and in anthologies. The historical precedent might be Mrs Siddons's 'Memorandum on the Character of Lady Macbeth' included in Campbell's *Life of Mrs Siddons*.

All contributors are, or have been, members of the Royal Shakespeare Company. A headnote to each essay offers selected details about each relevant production, with a little about the actor's Shakespearean career. The scripts have only been lightly edited and many informalities of style have been retained. References are to the *Riverside Shakespeare*, edited by G. Blakemore Evans, but the text is essentially that submitted by contributors and has miscellaneous, often modified, sources.

Acknowledgements

This book grows out of a Shakespeare Institute tradition of attentiveness to the theatre and its players. Although it is primarily the work of the actors, the Fellows of the Institute have variously contributed to its preparation and shaping. I am grateful to Tom Matheson, Robert Smallwood and Russell Jackson for assistance in planning the book, and for much advice and comment that I have tried to assimilate into the introduction. Lorna Flint provided the prefatory note to each essay and the Institute librarian, Susan Brock, solved many problems and reconstructed Malvolio's letter. Celia Charlesworth and Mavis Salmon patiently and resourcefully turned manuscripts, and some recorded talk, into typescript.

List of productions

Actor	Role	Play	Director	Theatre	Opening
Sinden	Malvolio	*Twelfth Night*	Barton	RST	21 August 1969
Suchet	Caliban	*Tempest*	Williams	RST	26 April 1978
Stewart	Shylock	*Merchant of Venice*	Barton	OP	3 May 1978
Rees	Posthumus	*Cymbeline*	Jones	RST	11–17 April 1979
Bowe	Orlando	*As You Like It*	Hands	RST	27 March 1980
Bruce	Nurse	*Romeo and Juliet*	Daniels	RST	16 April 1980
Pennington	Hamlet	*Hamlet*	Barton	RST	25 June 1980
Church	Polonius	*Hamlet*	Hall Barton	RST RST	19 August 1965 25 June 1980
Pasco	Timon	*Timon of Athens*	Daniels	OP	16 August 1980
Jones	Hermione	*Winter's Tale*	Eyre	RST	25 June 1981
Cusack	Portia	*Merchant of Venice*	Barton	RST	15 April 1981
Hutchings	Lavatch	*All's Well That Ends Well*	Nunn	RST	17 November 1981

Theatres

RST   The Royal Shakespeare Theatre, Stratford-upon-Avon
OP   The Other Place, Stratford-upon-Avon

Introduction:
abstracts and brief chronicles

PHILIP BROCKBANK

SHAKESPEARE'S PLAYS were written by an actor, and in a rich variety of senses they are actors' plays. It is the more surprising, therefore, that the present gathering of essays, studies and spontaneities appears to be the first of its kind. Readers and theatre-goers, whether critical or uncritical, ignorant or informed, have dominated the history of Shakespearean commentary, and actors have commonly had more opportunity to read about their own performances than to write about them. Not that innocent distinctions can for long be made between the play as read and the play as performed. All the players here have read and sometimes assiduously studied the plays and parts they acted, and they know better than most students or onlookers that a Shakespearean play is the sum of many possible readings and many possible performances.

Acting is necessary to life. The term 'role-playing' that sociologists have had to borrow from the language of the theatre recognizes the ubiquitous need to perform real or assumed social functions. Public suasion, in parliament or in the streets, Queen Elizabeth addressing the Commons or Antony in the Roman market-place, is invariably a form of theatre. And we keep the old Greek word for playing a part to describe the pervasive *hypocrisy* of society. 'Assume a virtue if you have it not', says Hamlet to Gertrude, inviting her to what we might call creative hypocrisy. Theatre has itself played a continuing but changing part in those processes of civilization that invite us to enjoy the game of assuming and anatomizing 'virtue' – the properties of being human.

There have been moments in Shakespearean history when it has been felt that knowledge and understanding could be stabilized and Shakespeare studies brought to an honourable end: editors could reconstruct authoritative texts, scholars recover the original conditions of the plays' creation, actors fully realize them in performance, and critics accurately tune the public's responses. While we must keep trying, we know we can't make it. At best 'we meet the past half-way' and what we make of its art, even of its facts, depends on what we are and are becoming. Thus Tony Church, playing Polonius over a span of decades, finds the role changing as he returns to it with different preoccupations, domestic and political. Changes are not always in a direction away from the past, however. It may well be that our present experience of Shakespeare's plays is closer to that of the audiences of his time than it has been for many generations. The masterpieces of art, including those of Greek and Renaissance theatre, keep recalling us to the understandings of the past. We now have a keener respect for Shakespeare's text than was usual on the stages of the eighteenth and nineteenth centuries, and our radical impulses in relation to the plays often turn out to be very conservative. Current interest in Shakespeare's self-conscious theatricality ('the art that displays art'), and in what is sometimes called 'meta-theatre', takes us back to pre-Shakespearean days when Erasmus wondered about the difference between a 'real' king and a player-king, and imagined the Olympians looking down on the human world, 'good god, what a theatre!'

Many have talked in recent years of 'the director's theatre'. In Shakespeare's time it is unlikely that there was such a presence as we now understand it, although the book-keeper might have assumed some of his minor functions. It is more appropriate to distinguish authentically between the actor's perspectives and the playwright's, and to see the relationship between actor and director as a reflection of that which in the days of the King's Men would have flourished between Shakespeare and the company. The players in the present collection usually speak affectionately, and only occasionally resistingly, about their directors. Since the directors have usually chosen their casts, this is unsurprising, but the courtesies do not disguise occasional tensions and divergences of purpose that no doubt had their counterpart in Shakespeare's own experience.

The actor's understanding of a play is likely to be very personal, that of the playwright less so. For the actor a character has an almost autonomous life, for the playwright a number of functions in a large design. Several players here (Rees, Pasco, Brenda Bruce) speak of their 'journey through the play', a metaphor (I am told) to which Peter Hall gave a certain currency. The actor needs a compass; the playwright makes a map and the director must read it. For the actor a play is a process to be lived through; for the playwright a structure to be assembled. But, as creative thinkers in the wake of Erasmus understood, if we think of characters as people then we must think correspondingly of the playwright as creator, designer, manipulator – disconcertingly like a god. Sometimes the invisible playwright and sometimes a visible *deus ex machina* descends to find solutions to human predicaments in the last act. Some people, of course, get away with behaving as if they were gods. Thus it happens that certain characters in Shakespeare's plays are allowed not merely the abilities of the actor but also some of the functions of the playwright. Richard of Gloucester, for example, who 'can change shapes with Proteus for advantages', is also, in effect, the principal plotter of his play, until Shakespeare and history see to it that he is over-reached. Similarly Edmund makes Edgar play a part in his play in *King Lear*, and Iago, another actor/playwright, dominates the plot of *Othello*. Two characters, the Duke in *Measure for Measure*, and Prospero in *The Tempest*, keep the play-maker's privileges to the very end, and their parts (one likes to think) could have appropriately been performed by Shakespeare himself.

It remains true, however, that characters can in some degree assume a momentum or life of their own, and take the playwrights or the director by surprise. Playing in his own plays, Shakespeare must have enjoyed this source of creative enterprise and tension (as when Barnardine refuses to die in *Measure for Measure*). The life of a part as distinct from its significance, is the prime responsibility of the actor, and actors have traditionally been suspicious of theory or analysis, ascribing the creation of character in performance to decisions instinctively made, perceptions unconsciously arrived at, fine discriminations mysteriously achieved. 'Analysis', said Michael Redgrave, 'does not come easily', and Roger Rees tells us that 'the act of making a character is a delicate thing, there are no rules'. The actor feels exposed and vulnerable, both in preparation and performance, feeling that his own personality and human resources are always on the line. In a sense it is so. Even spectators to a play or readers of a story are under imaginative pressure to find characters inside themselves, and are apt to come up against the boundaries of their own humanity. Hence a certain nervousness about type-casting – Roger Rees, for instance, feeling that his professional trajectory will take him from one character of 'failure' to another, from Aguecheek to Gayev in *The Cherry Orchard*. The actor's personal capacities and limitations are on display whether (to use a distinction made by Louis Jouvet) he is the *acteur*, moulding a character within the bounds of his own personality, or the *comédien* who by a protean creative process (perhaps in this respect like the author) becomes what he is not. Most of the actors represented here see themselves as *comédiens*, not so much subduing their personalities to a part as transcending them. Yet the sense of emotional and psychological risk remains acute. Thus Roger Rees,

3

attempting a soliloquy for the first time in his career, in the role of Posthumus, experienced a not uncharacteristic panic. Michael Pennington is witness to the greater strain on the actor's own personality in attempting Hamlet. 'The main challenge', he writes, 'is to express fully the deep crises of the part through your own spirit.' 'This is where the part shakes you like a rat', he says of one moment in the play, and 'I was beginning to taste the famous isolation of the part, feeling the emotional tides of a man adrift from the behaviour, the humour, the very language of his neighbours: a disorientation that in some equivalent way was beginning to separate me from colleagues and friends.'

The sensitivities of the actor, therefore, are likely to become entangled with the complex stresses created in the character. And *Hamlet* is, of all Shakespeare's plays, the one that most searchingly anatomizes the actor and is most intimately engaged with 'actions that a man might play', with (as we have had reason to notice) the hypocrisies of the kingdom, the truth that a man might 'smile and smile, and be a villain'. The capacity to act out the killing of the king waits not only upon 'occasion' or outward circumstance, but also on 'that within which passes show'. Not Shakespeare alone, but also a literary tradition and the experience of the live theatre of his time, made the play *Hamlet*, and it is about the possibility of transforming a 'rotten' Denmark not only by 'acting' appropriately but also by making plays that 'hold the mirror up to nature'. Hamlet too is an actor turned playwright, seeking to make a play that contains his own role in a larger scene. But ironically, as many have observed, and as many playing the part must have found out for themselves, Hamlet's surgery exposes himself as well as the society. It is, for example, an ironic truth that in his 'mousetrap' play Lucianus is both Hamlet ('nephew to the king') and Claudius (pouring poison in the king's ear). Renaissance art was very sensitive to the relationship between structures of society and structures of the 'self' (although this is a modern way of putting it). Michael Pennington, rehearsing and performing Hamlet, is not only turning himself over, he is re-enacting a phase of history.

The same might be said of Patrick Stewart playing Shylock or Richard Pasco taking on the related role of Timon of Athens. But some actors are more aware than others of the nature of their engagement with the 'self' and with the 'past'. Stewart gives a very precise account of reactions to historical and stage traditions of the theatre Jew, and is prepared to offer details of the solutions he found to the actor's moral, psychological and technical problems. Pasco keeps in retrospect at a certain distance from his own performance, preferring to give a general account of the play and of his responses to it. In practice his performance, like Michael Pennington's, varied through the course of the production – sometimes quiet and intense, sometimes more aggressive and shrill. Much depends upon what comes back from the audience.

The tensions generated by the actor's committed self, living the part in performance, taking off from the moment, finding the audience and the other players, were familiar to the great actors of the past, and they stirred the spectators to an answering experience:

Though pit, gallery, and boxes were crowded to suffocation, the chill of the grave seemed about you while you looked at her; there was the hush and damp of the charnel-house at midnight . . . Your flesh crept and your breathing became uneasy.

Perhaps Sheridan Knowles, who reported Mrs Siddons as Lady Macbeth, had been reading too many Gothick novels; 'Well sir', he goes on, 'I smelt blood! I swear I smelt blood!' But Mrs Siddons's creative communion with the character remained in some way detached, and was made by rigorous discipline, careful preparation and even by discursive analysis (see her 'Memorandum on the Character of Lady Macbeth' in Campbell's *Life*, 1834). Yet Fanny Kemble could claim later that Siddons's true analysis was in the performance, not in the memorandum. It is good now to have the one when we can no longer have the other; but both have a contribution to make to our understanding. We have to accept that the transient occasion will elude systematic account, for as Pennington says:

An individual performance . . . is a live thing, with its own conditions and unpredictability; and to an extent the actor, given a base of discipline and control, must allow himself to be carried by the prevailing winds. Everyone wants the occasion to be special; everyone, including the actors, waits for lightning to strike.

The lightning strikes only when the appropriate charges induce it. The conditions of the special occasion are created by exhaustive preparation both of the text and of the actor's self (or selves), while the audience waits in its own state of preparation and alertness.

An unacknowledged presence behind virtually all of the actors' accounts here, thoroughly assimilated, it would seem, into the English tradition, is Stanislavski's *An Actor Prepares*. He puts the essential point a little romantically:

Our type of creativeness is the conception and birth of a new being – the person in the part. It is a natural act similar to the birth of a human being.

'Creativeness', he says, 'is not a technical trick . . . It is not an external portrayal of images and passions.' But Stanislavski was aware that techniques must nevertheless be acquired. Sometimes we think we know when an actor is merely mechanical in his effects; but it is also likely that we are often deceived into supposing spontaneous or improvised, effects that are carefully calculated (see, for example, John Bowe's account of his fall into the auditorium from the wrestling in *As You Like It*).

For all the tuning to the high and special occasion, and the arduous personal preparation required from the actor, there are strong continuities of acting tradition, and particular productions often reach a poised (though still lively) state, in which many performances bring few surprises. Theatre depends upon meeting expectations as well as on frustrating them. As audiences we wish to be reassured of our own convivial humanity as well as to be hurried on to new possibilities. It is both satisfying and exciting to be suspended on the boundaries of the predictable and the unpredictable. That tension is a little like that between actor and playwright. When, in *The Tempest*, Trinculo and Stephano are distracted by 'glistering apparel' it is as if Shakespeare has diverted his players to the wardrobe, just as they are out to stop him having everything his own way. The 'trumpery' in Prospero's house (Shakespeare's theatre) is 'stale to catch thieves'.

Chaucer's characters, said Blake, 'are the physiognomies or lineaments of universal human life, beyond which Nature never steps'. It is an extravagant expression of the truth that we are quick to recognize, and to conform to, certain types known (as in the *Canterbury Tales*) by their physiognomy, their humours, their professions or callings, or even by their characteristic diseases. It is possible sometimes to see an actor composing his character from what is, after all, a limited stock of possibilities. Thus Donald Sinden's Malvolio is 'vertical', with a domed head and a military demeanour; while Geoffrey Hutchings's Lavatch is given a physical handicap (a stoop, after trying a hump) which dramatizes his alienation. An actor, particularly a comic actor, has often to contend with a strong tradition of stage characterization which he can best use by resisting. Thus Patrick Stewart is up against audience expectations of Shylock:

So strong is this image of the Jew with the raised weapon that in rehearsals I had to resist the impulse to menace Antonio in this way, and throughout the life of the production I felt secretly guilty that I was denying the audience their right to see this traditional tableau.

Not only the need to cultivate the kind of innocence from which fresh responses can be generated, but also the drive towards novelty and originality of interpretation, invites the actor to break the moulds of the past.

Yet it cannot be easy for an actor to distinguish, even to his own satisfaction, between tradition and innovation. Many of the effects that Donald Sinden played for in his 1969 Malvolio (the rotation on the word 'revolve' when he reads the letter, and his unaccustomed and laboured 'run' at Olivia's command) have long been, and continue to be, moments of audience expectation. His shocked repetition of the word 'run', however, and his witty play with the stage properties were innovations strictly for the occasion.

There is little trace in these essays of the belief the French have sometimes entertained in 'la seule inflexion juste'. The English would appear to be confident that there can be new, valid readings, that the text is open to many alternative possibilities, and that there is no definitive reading or production. Much of this confidence is owed specifically to the open mystery of Shakespeare's art, which is rich in ambiguous effects, resonances and references, often refusing to let the language say one thing at a time. The term 'subtext' was used by Stanislavski about 'the inwardly felt expression of a human being in a part, which flows uninterruptedly beneath the words of the text, giving them life and a basis for existing'. Many contributors here use the method and some use the term, but in differing degrees and ways. Gemma Jones, for example, spending her time in the super-market or on a London bus 'thinking pregnant' as she approached the playing of Hermione, was in search of the subtext. Donald Sinden, who uses the word, keeps up (once for the sake of the playing, now for the sake of the exposition) a running commentary of unspoken words and thoughts. He reports that Trevor Nunn allowed him to vocalize the word 'run' (once vetoed by John Barton) with the remark, 'it *is* in the subtext'. Brenda Bruce and David Suchet comb the text to find in the roles of others, as well as in their own, the clues and the evidence that assist their re-creations. Brenda Bruce uses an angry speech by Capulet to serve as her 'subtext', and David Suchet from a dozen points of the play assembles his figure of Caliban. 'Subtext' should not, I suspect, be used to elicit words which ought to be in the text and aren't, but 'the flow beneath the words' is probably an indispensable dynamic in the actor's achieved performance. Some cultivate it (or its illusion) in their own lives outside the theatre, or in the imagined life of the character outside the play (see Sinden on Malvolio and Hutchings on Lavatch). In Shakespeare's plays, however, there is another mode of 'subtext' generated by the turbulent obliquities of the language. When Claudius, for example, tells Laertes of Hamlet's return to Denmark he says, 'But to the quick of the ulcer Hamlet comes back'; the phrase means 'to get to the point', but at a changed pace it tells us that Hamlet returns to the centre of corruption. The performances of Michael Pennington and Richard Pasco showed them sensitive to such verbal latencies.

From the evidence before us it would seem that some actors are more attentive than others to relationships between characters and to the play as a whole. Sinead Cusack, for example, who enjoyed imagining scenes outside the play, gives a lot of attention to her relationships with Shylock and Bassanio, finding herself more satisfied with her playing of the bond-plot than of the love-plot. She also shows herself more than usually aware of possibilities other than those which the production brought to life. There is always a performed play in each production and a number of unperformed ones remaining on the page. Sinead Cusack, after successfully realizing a melancholy and anxious Portia, is left eager to play a more buoyant version.

While there are many possible performances, there are also impossible ones, and diverse potentials are worked out within real, if hard to define, boundaries. The criteria of characterization are not merely subjective, they can grow out of historical understanding and out of analysis of the public world. Tony Church, playing Polonius in 1965, tells us that he had one eye on Burghley, Shakespeare's contemporary, and the other on Harold Macmillan, his own. This openness, and the player's alertness to our contemporary world, help to transform theatre history from the inert weight of custom it might otherwise be into a rich inheritance. New performances can take off from the old and can change their significance. Tony Church's larger view of the play and its changing cultural contexts affects the detailed realization of particular speeches:

At the end of the advice Polonius says: 'This above all, to thine own self be true: And it must follow, as the night the day, Thou canst not then be false to any man.' In the 1965 production I had delivered those lines as a direct appeal to naked self-interest; in 1980 I spoke them as a simple moral truth which I knew my son would share with me.

There is much in his account, and in others, to suggest that acting, like the life it expresses, calls for a great range of inward and outward observations, some momentous and others apparently trivial.

Brenda Bruce played in a production of *Romeo and Juliet*, directed by Ron Daniels and clearly addressed to an audience aware of the present condition of Northern Ireland: 'The children, carrying their elders' bitterness and aggression and bigotry into the streets, fight and kill each other.' The problem for Brenda Bruce's Nurse was to meet and stand up to the 'leather-clad, greasy-haired, menacing' figures in the street, for the audience 'was not prepared to laugh at the ill-treatment of Nurse':

Since by now we knew each other rather well and trusted each other as actors, we agreed to improvise the next night. The boys were light and frivolous and I *enjoyed* their fun. Instead of using my fan to make a ladylike image, I hit them about their heads. It was a Japanese paper fan and made a sharp noise. The audience laughed. After three slaps they laughed and clapped. After a few performances the fan broke and the prop boys substituted another fan. It was short and the ribs were made of plastic, instead of cane. When I hit the boys the smart crack was missing. The wonderful tingle of comedy-timing disappeared. On my free days I drove to all the Japanese emporiums from Oxford to East Finchley in search of the correct fan, without much luck.

The apparently trifling detail had its place in a performance which made the most of the Nurse's energy and life-delight, and of her ability to cope with a world that keeps pulling itself apart.

The players in *Romeo and Juliet* (and indeed in any of Shakespeare's plays) are engaged not only in living the life of the character but also in demonstrating the processes that are changing a whole community of characters – in this instance, the city of Verona. The audience's feelings are engaged, but not their personal, intimate feelings only, but also collective ones, shared with, and picked up from, our neighbours in the theatre. We have one kind of concern for the lovers and another kind for the city. Looked at one way, the actor and the audience correspond with the individual and the society; but looked at another, the actor is seeking from the audience sometimes a private and sometimes a public response, sometimes speaking man-to-man and sometimes man-to-mass. Bertolt Brecht did much to return European traditions of theatre to public and social modes of thought and feeling, but in England the communal styles have not, from present evidence, displaced those techniques of empathy and illusion practised, for example, by the player of Priam in the court of Elsinore. Michael Pennington's Hamlet, holding the player's mask, nicely expresses the distance, and the nearness, from one mode to the other.

The true test of the players' alertness to their contemporary world is, ultimately, their control of an audience. Sinead Cusack tells a revealing story of the actor's sensitivity to straying attention; but the most measurable of audience signals is laughter for which Donald Sinden, on this occasion, attempts a digital rating. On other occasions (for example, in his performance of Lear) Sinden has used his quick audience-rapport to tragic effect. Playing for laughs and playing for effect have their risks, and in the history of Shakespearean theatre some of the loudest laughs and hottest splashing tears have been improperly solicited – by intrusions of stage business and even of fake text (see Hamlet's advice to the players). The keenest and most searching effects, however, are won from the text, often by carefully rehearsed timing. It is important, for example, that Orlando should enter carrying the exhausted Adam, precisely at the line, 'Sans teeth, sans eyes, sans taste, sans everything'.

Some actors concern themselves very fully with the edited text and with the scholarship of the play. David Suchet is very attentive to punctuation, for example, and both he and Geoffrey Hutchings look for historical warrant for their rendering of a character's appearance. The preparation of a role, even before rehearsals start, can take many weeks. But over the rehearsal period (usually in the Royal Shakespeare Company about six weeks) there can of course be many new and fundamental discoveries, often owed to interplay of character. Hutchings, for example, found that Lavatch's relationship with the Countess was crucially important. Had another performer played the Countess the effect might have been different; for it is not improbable that his sense of Lavatch's 'clairvoyant' understanding with her was owed to his acting-rapport with Peggy Ashcroft.

There are perhaps a thousand characters in Shakespeare's plays, including Innogen, wife to Leonato in *Much Ado*, who never says a word, and Isbel, Lavatch's sweetheart who, it seems, may be a private joke. It is the business of the actor to re-create them, and to entertain us with the prospect of more and richer ways of being human. These essays are intended as glimpses behind the scenes for those who know that illusions are shaped from realities, that feelings are evoked by art, and that hard work informs the actors' playing of an actor's plays.

Shylock in
The Merchant of Venice
PATRICK STEWART

PATRICK STEWART is an Associate Artist of the Royal Shakespeare Company, and has developed his stage career within the company since 1966. At the same time, he has made a number of films and has become known to a wide audience through his extensive work in television – notably as the doctor in the *Maybury* series. At Stratford, he has appeared in both modern and classic roles, and his range within Shakespeare is wide. In 1967, for instance, he played both Grumio and Duke Senior; in 1968, both Cornwall and Touchstone; in 1970 both King John and Launce. His Enobarbus in the 1978 production of *Antony and Cleopatra* won him in 1979 the Society of West End Theatre Award for Best Supporting Actor. In view of his versatility, it was scarcely surprising that in 1981 Patrick Stewart not only played Leontes but also, in the double bill of *The Two Gentlemen of Verona* and *Titus Andronicus*, both Sir Eglamour and Titus. His most recent appearance for the Royal Shakespeare Company has been at the Barbican where he played the King in both parts of *King Henry IV*. His performance of Shylock was in a production at The Other Place in 1978, directed by John Barton and designed by Christopher Morley.

'Shylock, in *The Merchant of Venice*, can be played as a wolfish villain, sadistically lusting for the blood of a Christian he hates. Or, he can be interpreted as a dignified symbol of an oppressed people intellectually and morally superior to the Christians who taunt and abuse him.' So began one review of John Barton's production of *The Merchant of Venice* when it opened in London in May 1979. The production was then a year old, having opened in Stratford in the previous spring, and I had been playing Shylock almost continuously since then. At the time, the depressing narrowness of this critic's view of the role appalled me, but had I been more objective, I might have recalled there had been a time when I would have shared this blinkered view.

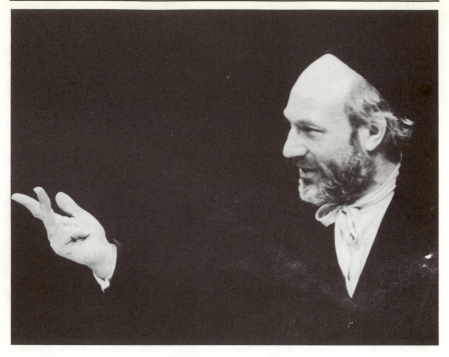

1 'This kindness will I show'
Patrick Stewart as Shylock, May 1979

The prospect of rehearsing Shylock had not excited me. On the day the part was offered I had felt an irritable disappointment that my principal role in the 1978 season might only be Shylock in *The Merchant of Venice*, rather than a challenging role in a greater play. I had played the part thirteen years earlier. That experience, and other later contacts with the play, had soured my feelings in such a way that I too could only see Shylock as a racial symbol, serving the play with either of these two clichéd faces; inhibited by gentile timidity, and uneasy and ambivalent feelings about the alleged racist nature of the *Merchant*, only the sentimental interpretation would seem to be tolerable; and that prospect was only marginally more tiresome than the melodramatic alternative. Not an appealing prospect, to be trapped in the straitjacket of a rigid and predetermined characterization, suspecting that the part could only be made distinctive and vivid through effects, and faced with all that 'my daughter and my ducats' acting; not 'owning' the play, nor dominating it. Shylock is a curious role, in that its fame and reputation are quite out of proportion with his share of the lines. He appears in only five scenes and two of these are very brief. There have been occasions when producers and actor-managers, reacting perhaps to the feeling that the part needed 'expanding', have added a sixth scene. The scene which might be called 'Shylock's return' was played after Act 2, Scene 6 and shows Shylock arriving home to find his house bereft of daughter, jewels and ducats. Past productions have developed this scene in different ways. Irving played it very tastefully. A solitary figure crossing a bridge, reaching the door of his house, knocking and waiting in lonely silence as the curtain falls. Thirty years later Herbert Beerbohm Tree had a livelier approach. As Toby Lelyveld reports:

When Shylock returns home, to find Jessica and his money gone, he bursts into the house, rages through its rooms and appearing now at this window and now at that, cries out the name of his daughter in a crescendo, until he at last collapses. [Then he came] dashing out of doors; he flung himself on the ground, and tore his garments and sprinkled ashes on his head.　　　　　(*Shylock on the Stage*, 1961, p. 100)

Shylock's role is also diminished by his having no appearance in Act 5 and some have resolved this by ending the play with his exit from the trial.

One of the intriguing pleasures of performing a long role, particularly in Shakespeare, is to feel oneself as the heartbeat of the play; not only caught up in the rhythmic surging movement of the play's energy, but to be the energy itself, the pulse. Like riding a powerful horse, in performance the actor feels the reins of the play, holding in or giving head as the story moves forward, and the control never being applied in quite the same way twice. For the actor playing Shylock this control is never possible as he spends more time waiting his turn to mount than actually riding in the saddle.

However, it was not Shylock's limited share of the play and his stereotyped function that were discouraging for an actor looking for rich, human complexities; there is even a stereotyped image that goes with the part – swarthy, foreign features (invariably incorporating a prominent hooked nose), ringlets, eastern robes (rich or shabby to taste) and clutching either the famous scales or the murderous knife. So strong is this image of the Jew with the raised weapon that in rehearsals I had to resist the impulse to menace Antonio in this way, and throughout the life of the production I felt secretly guilty that I was denying the audience their right to see this traditional tableau. I think it was this sense of so much tradition attached to the role that was uninspiring, and the fear of finding oneself trundling along tramlines, trapped in a lifeless mould. Nevertheless, actor's curiosity, the mysterious reputation of the role and the appeal of Shakespeare in the small space of The Other Place was finally sufficient reason for accepting the part. And so I found myself on the threshold of an experience that was for two years to be entirely fascinating and very rewarding.

At my first meeting with the play's director, John Barton, he spoke briefly of his feelings about the play and its characters but he said it was a 'cool' play, a fairy story, and he talked of a sense of melancholy threaded through it. Music would be very important, he said (James Walker's lovely score was a marvellous unifier of the play). He and the designer, Christopher Morley, had decided to adapt the auditorium of The Other Place into a 'theatre in the round', thus making a set unnecessary and destroying, at a stroke, one *Merchant of Venice* cliché, the bridge and gondola backdrop. As for Shylock, his brief was very simple – he must be a monster. At my first reading I had been delighted to discover how marvellously witty Shylock was, particularly in the early part of the play, and so suggested he might be an entertaining monster, and so we 'shook hands and a bargain'. Finally, and with some firmness, John Barton said that he felt that the play had for too long belonged to Shylock (so much for all the above), and that this production should restore an equal balance between Bassanio, Shylock and Portia.

My homework begins with reading the play – contriving an innocence if the play is familiar – setting my imagination free to react intuitively and simply to whatever the reading suggests. After a long rehearsal period, when the play has been so dismantled and probed that the simple elements, such as the story-line, or the bold outlines of a character or of a relationship, have become blurred or submerged with elaboration and detail, it is valuable to remind oneself of those first uncomplicated responses.

In 1.3 Shylock jokes with Bassanio and lightens their opening discussion with a series of puns – though rather bad ones.

SHYLOCK   Antonio is a good man.
BASSANIO   Have you heard any imputation to the contrary?
SHYLOCK   Ho, no, no, no, no! My meaning in saying he is a good man is to have you
      understand me that he is sufficient.   (1.3.12–17)

Like an experienced comic Shylock sets up Bassanio with his 'good man' and Bassanio will indignantly rise to the bait, only for Shylock to prick his pompous bubble with innocent laughter, and his explanation of his commercial use of 'good'. Then again, Shylock plays on words in, 'There be land rats . . . pirates', and in his reply to Bassanio's 'Be assured you may' – 'I will be assured I may.' His highly tuned, ironic sense of double meanings, his use of language as a weapon or a smoke-screen or an analgesic, present an insight into his character. Possibly his wit provides a way of ingratiating himself with the Christian businessmen, and the irony protects him from the humiliation of being an alien, without losing his self-respect. Does it also suggest this could be someone speaking in a language which is not his own but which he has so carefully assimilated that, like many naturalized foreigners, he uses it better than the natives? He certainly employs a colourful and at times bizarre turn of phrase – particularly the Jacob/Laban speech in 1.3 – and this persuaded me not to use a 'foreign' accent, as it seemed that the nature of his language itself set him apart. Shylock's good humour is still present after Antonio has entered in 1.3:

> ANTONIO   Was this inserted to make interest good?
>   Or is your gold and silver ewes and rams?
> SHYLOCK   I cannot tell, I make it breed as fast.   (1.3.94–6)

And in the speech where Shylock describes Antonio's treatment of him, from 'what should I say to you', Shylock, with delicious mockery, is turning Antonio's insults back on him.

During my early work on the play I was strongly influenced by a theme that runs throughout but is particularly marked in the early scenes. Images of money, commerce and possessions abound, and even people seem to have a price. The value of assets and possessions always seems to dominate and colour relationships. This theme, where it touches Shylock, appears as a series of alternatives for comparison. People, feeling, religion and race versus commerce and material security. Shylock's choices are surprising but – with one exception – consistent. This evidence, and what it seemed to indicate about his personality, became the foundation for my characterization of Shylock. The principal moments of choice were these, in 1.3:

> I hate him for he is a Christian;
> But more, for that in low simplicity
> He lends out money gratis and brings down
> The rate of usance here with us in Venice . . .
> He hates our sacred nation and he rails
> Even there where merchants most do congregate
> On me, my bargains, and my well won thrift,
> Which he calls interest.   (1.3.42–51)

Then in 3.1 where Shylock, who has been discussing the loss of his daughter, hears of Antonio's commercial loss, and lumps the two together as 'another bad match':

He hath disgraced me and hindered me half a million, laughed at my losses, mocked at my gains, scorned my nation, thwarted my bargains, cooled my friends, heated mine enemies; and what's his reason?   (3.1.54–8)

Only one point in Shylock's list of Antonio's wrongs touches on race and religion. The rest is business.

TUBAL   I often came where I did hear of her but cannot find her.
SHYLOCK   Why, there, there, there, there! A diamond gone, cost me two thousand
   ducats in Frankfort!   (3.1.81–5)

Shylock is mourning not for the lost daughter, but for the lost diamond:

I would my daughter were dead at my foot, and the jewels in her ear. Would she were
hears'd at my foot, and the ducats in her coffin!   (3.1.87–90)

Shylock's wish to punish his daughter and to remove her shame by having her dead is at one with the return of his valuables:

I will have the heart of him if he forfeit, for were he out of Venice I can make what
merchandise I will.   (3.1.127–9)

Shylock's justification of Antonio's death is solely and ruthlessly commercial:

You take my life
When you do take the means whereby I live.   (4.1.376–7)

With three simple words – 'I am content' – Shylock agrees that half his fortune should be put in trust for Jessica and Lorenzo, that he should bequeath his estate to them at his death, and that he should at once become a Christian.

A picture emerges of a man in whose life there is an imbalance, an obsession with the retention and acquisition of wealth which is so fixated that it displaces the love and paternal feelings of father for daughter. It transcends race and religion and is felt to be as important as life itself. It inhibits warm, affectionate responses and isolates him from his fellow man. There is a bleak and terrible loneliness in Shylock which I suspect is the cause of much of his anger and bitterness. This sense of loneliness and how he copes with it became increasingly important to me throughout the life of this production. Indeed, there were occasions when its presence became almost dangerously overwhelming. Of course, it is not loneliness that the actor *shows*, but its compensating aspects: false gregariousness, ingratiating humour, violence and arrogance. Whatever the circumstance of his situation, scene by scene Shylock always stands in isolation. Until, that is, in 4.1 when a young doctor from Rome stands with him and seems to take his part. Shylock trusts this support and suffers for it. But if Shylock's nature is distorted by avarice, what is the cause? A man does not spring into the world unhappy, cruel and mean. It is his experience of the world, its treatment of him and his attempts to cope, that shape and form or bend and warp him. Shylock and his kind are outsiders, strangers, feared and hated for being different. They belong to the world's minorities. They are, as the laws of Venice state, alien, stamped by that world to be always vulnerable and at risk; therefore survival is paramount. Shylock is a survivor. He has clung to life in Venice and he has prospered. The alien's methods of survival in a suspicious and hostile environment are many. He can go underground and disappear. He can establish a bold and confident public reputation – a dangerous method. He can abandon all aspects of himself that set him apart and develop a new and conforming identity. Shylock, I believe, has found a way of merging with his surroundings, shabby and unmemorable, and, if he attracts attention at all, appearing as an eccentric and harmless clown. Only Antonio, his competitor in business whose senses are sharpened by commerce, smells the contempt that hides behind Shylock's jokes.

A further aid to survival is money. It will purchase favours and friends, build a wall of protection, buy silence and, in the hardest times, help to maintain a grip on life. It can also create a multitude of dependencies which, being impossible to unravel, will prove a true security. In the twelfth century the Jews in England were extremely useful in the economic scheme. Lelyveld says:

> [They] paid one half of King Richard's 100,000 marks ransom, while the entire city of London was assessed only 1,500 marks. In order to finance the Third Crusade, the Jews . . . were taxed to the extent of one-fourth of their movable property, while the remainder of the population paid one-tenth. Although the Jews constituted only one quarter of one per-cent of the total population . . . they contributed eight per-cent of the total income of the treasury. (*Shylock on the Stage*, p. 5)

Shylock has perhaps known the vulnerability of poverty – maybe the memory of Leah is linked with it – and from that experience has grown the determination to forge a material security which has, through years of bitter compromise and humiliation, grown into the wretched obsession that possesses Shylock at the start of the play. A feature of this obsession could be excessive meanness. Lancelot claims that he is famished in Shylock's service and in this production he might be believed, as he appeared severely undernourished. Shylock's notion of gourmandizing might be merely the satisfying of youthful appetite. In 2.5, which was set inside Shylock's house, the lighting was so dim as to suggest that most of the lightbulbs, or rather candles, had been removed. As this production was set towards the end of the nineteenth century it allowed the use of modern props to help establish location, create mood and define character – playing-cards, toy pistols, champagne, cigars and cigarettes. Antonio smoked cheroots, Tubal a havana, and Shylock his mean little hand-rolled cigarettes, whose butt-ends were safely stored away for future use. This meanness was carried over into Shylock's appearance which showed an almost studied contempt for neatness or even cleanliness. A shabby black frock coat, torn at the hem and stained, a waistcoat dusted with cigarette ash, baggy black trousers, short in the leg, exposing down-at-heel old boots, and a collarless shirt yellowing with age. Apart from the yarmulke, the only other distinctive garment was a yellow sash, twisted round the waist and only just visible beneath the waistcoat. This ritual-like garment and its wearing was an invention of the designer's, though based on photographs of Russian Jews in the nineteenth century, who wore a yellow sash over a long frock coat. We wanted to avoid any excessive sense of Jewishness or foreignness in appearance but this detail, almost unnotice-able in the earlier scenes could, in the court, be boldly worn over the frock coat as a proud demonstration of Shylock's racial difference.

In the early scenes, however, I was anxious to minimize the impression of Shylock's Jewishness. Whenever I had seen either a very ethnic or detailedly Jewish Shylock I felt that something was lost. Jewishness could become a smoke-screen which might conceal both the particular and the universal in the role. See him as a Jew first and foremost and he is in danger of becoming only a symbol, although a symbol that has changed over the centuries as society's attitudes have changed.

Toby Lelyveld traces the role through from the beginning. For the Elizabethans Shylock's outrageous behaviour came as no shock, and for many years he was played 'in the vein of the lowest comedy'. After the 'stormy and diabolical Shylock' of Macklin, Kean broke tradition 'and re-created the character as a persecuted martyr, forced by circumstance to become an avenger'. Irving's Shylock was marked by 'intense pathos and a keen sense of injury', and the role began to assume its tragic intensity. Over the years, however, Irving's 'early humanitarian treatment coarsened', and the obsessive, sneering avenger returned to the stage. In the nineteen-twenties and thirties, *The Merchant* was produced three times at the Old Vic and on each occasion an attempt was made to focus attention away from Shylock, the bond-plot subordinated to the fairy tale. In 1932 Malcolm Keen's 'realistic and powerful' Shylock was 'not allowed to dominate the action'. And when John Gielgud, who had directed Keen, played the part himself in 1938, he showed himself still determined 'to keep the play from becoming the tragedy of the Jew'.

Because of the Nazis' Final Solution and six million deaths, those passages of anti-semitic expression in *The Merchant* will reverberate powerfully for any audience in this second half of the twentieth century. Actor and director will not need to emphasize them, nor must they be avoided. An audience must witness the intolerance of Antonio, the shallowness of Bassanio, the boorishness of Gratiano and the cynicism of Lorenzo. The unease we feel at these characterizations is important. It complicates these men who are at the heart of the romantic story of *The Merchant*, makes us less happy to accept them or not question their motives. Indeed there is an ambivalence in every corner of the play, so that no matter how well a director may bathe Act 5 in the lyrical wash of romance and fairy tale, the memories of cruelty, dishonesty and selfishness will cast troubling shadows across the Belmont dawn. But however important Jewishness and anti-semitism are in the play they are secondary to the consideration of Shylock, the man: unhappy, unloved, lonely, frightened and angry. And no matter how monstrous his cold-blooded attempt on Antonio's life, it is the brave, insane solitary act of a man who will defer no more, compromise no more. Taking Antonio's life is his line of no retreat and, although justified on commercial grounds, this murder is also, therefore, symbolic. Perhaps this makes of Shylock a revolutionary in modern terms. Certainly, when as Shylock I stood in the court and said 'my deeds upon my head', I felt closer to *all* those oppressed and abused who stand up in the face of a hostile and powerful enemy. This was not one Jew, but all victims who turn on their persecutors. It is in this sense that it seems Shakespeare created a portrait of an outsider who happened to be a Jew. But of course Shylock does step back from the line, he does compromise, he settles for a deal, and the patient shrug once more copes with humiliation. In the humble compliance of 'I am content' and 'send the deed after me and I will sign it', Shakespeare's massive understanding touches the harsh, unsentimental facts of survival. However, this is at the end of the Shylock story, and I would like now to look at that story in more detail, noting the major objectives, the motivations, thought processes and imaginative associations that lay behind one actor's interpretation.

Shylock appears in five scenes. Each scene has a quite distinctive quality. One approach would be to blend these qualities in such a way as to present a regular and consistent picture at all appearances. On the other hand, the particular characteristics of each scene can be isolated and individually played without reference to other scenes. This approach relies on the conviction that it will not be until the moment of his final exit that the last piece will be added to the puzzle that is Shylock, and the picture completed and truly consistent. I have said that the first scene is rich in humour. There is an extravert energy in Shylock. He is garrulous, friendly and entirely reasonable. Even before the scene begins, however, Shylock's arrival is anticipated, almost ominously, by Portia's last words at the end of the preceding scene. 'Whiles we shut the gates upon one wooer, another knocks at the door.' Shylock is not a wooer but Portia's apprehension is well-founded, as the next person we shall see will be the play's villain. Perhaps there lies in 'knocks at the door' a suggestion as to how '3,000 ducats' should be said. It seems probable that in the offstage dialogue Bassanio has explained the details of the loan and now Shylock is having him repeat it over, giving no answer but teasing him with each repeated 'well'. There is too a sense of surprise and pleasure in being approached by Bassanio and Antonio, though this is certainly a pretence.

But the speech about Antonio's sufficiency must impress Bassanio with Shylock's knowledge of the merchant's business and the risks involved in maritime trading. This speech is also an opportunity to demonstrate Shylock's quickness of thought and agility with language. He picks up his cues eagerly, often impatient for the other character to finish. It is an indicator of his bright intelligence. I saw no sign in the text that he is deliberate, pedantic or ponderous in his speech. Everything points to speed and liveliness. There is more humour in the 'pork' speech. A joke about 'the Nazarites' and a polite little lecture about the dietary and religious laws of the Jews. This speech is often played as hostile and aggressive, but why risk antagonizing Bassanio when there are so many intriguing possibilities behind this encounter? Antonio arrives and we move from prose to verse. The contenders are face to face; the tone of the scene shifts and becomes more tense. Verse is needed now, and the change of rhythm must be apparent in Shylock's aside. Here are no games, no jokes, but bitterness and resentment. It is a speech to the audience, therefore the truth, and they should be shocked to see this change. Shakespeare permits the audience to taste Shylock's real feelings so that they will see through the play-acting that is to follow. It is interesting that Antonio begins by justifying his involvement in this deal. It is for a friend, but he is clearly embarrassed. This makes him vulnerable and Shylock knows it. So the teasing and the mockery begin. The Jacob speech is very characteristic of Shylock. A colourful and witty justification of thrift and sharp dealing. Shylock also plays the 'amusing story-teller' but Antonio is not amused. His response is crude and insulting. Has Shylock merited 'devil', 'evil soul', 'villain', 'rotten at the heart' and 'falsehood'? Here is a sure sign of Antonio's discomfort and embarrassment. How does Shylock react? He tells us in the next speech. A patient shrug and back to the matter in hand. But Shylock's passive acceptance is a goad to Antonio and he angrily demands an answer. Shylock's response is a masterly piece of controlled and brilliant irony. He is saying: 'Signor Antonio, I am puzzled. You abuse me for the way I make my living and I understand that, and can put up with it. But now I am confused because you want my professional help and I don't know how I should react to you. Please tell me what is right, what I should do.' Antonio cannot live with that level of complexity and he clubs his way back to a simple hostility that makes him feel secure. Shylock, still sympathetic, talks of friendship and love, but baits his hook with mention of an interest-free loan. And still the puns continue: 'This is kind I offer.' Bassanio, quick to sense something for nothing, bites. And Shylock, in one swiftly flowing, innocently spontaneous sentence, delivers the final mock of the flesh bond. And mockery is all it is. Shylock, knowing the extent of Antonio's wealth, could not dream that he would fail so dramatically. He will help his enemy but his hatred will publicly show itself in the humiliating clause of the pound of flesh. Shylock teases them about their suspicions and daringly inserts a final mock about the flesh of muttons, beefs and goats being more estimable than Antonio's. For most of the scene the audience should have enjoyed watching him enjoying himself. Here is an entertaining eccentric we look forward to seeing again. Before his exit a private shadow passes across Shylock as he mentions his house and this shadow will soon blot out the cheeriness of 1.3.

2.5 is Shylock's most private scene. The others are public, and as such, Shylock is on show, conscious of onlookers and the effect he is having. In 2.5 there is no need for a public face and the unrestrained man will emerge. There are only two references to life in Shylock's house, and though they come from different people they are complementary, and present an appalling picture: 'The Jew my master is a kind of devil', 'The very devil incarnation', 'I am famished in his service.' Jessica says simply and bleakly 'Our house is hell.' This, I felt, is the description that 2.5 has to live up to. It is not the hell of poverty or meanness or even cruelty, but the hell of a house from which love has been withdrawn. This is the hell that Jessica flees from to give herself to the (questionable) love of Lorenzo. Young Gobbo is leaving to work for Bassanio and is sneered and snarled at while

Jessica is called with an impatience that grows dangerous. Jessica is treated like an incompetent servant, and the mention of masques releases Shylock's suppressed, sour anger, the anger of resentment – resentments of a lifetime that each day grow more bitter. Only within the walls of his home can this anger be released. The joker of 1.3 is here appalled at the thought of the drum and the fife, and in 5.1 Lorenzo tells Jessica that

> The man that hath no music in himself,
> Nor is not moved with concord of sweet sounds,
> Is fit for treasons, stratagems and spoils;
> The motions of his spirit are dull as night,
> And his affections dark as Erebus:
> Let no such man be trusted. (5.1.83–8)

There is violence in Shylock as well as anger, and it ripples below the surface of this domestic scene. Perhaps Shylock sees in Jessica's eyes something of her inexplicable defiance and her intended escape. I saw it and struck at her face in anger and frustration – painful and humiliating for her and for Shylock. 'Perhaps I will return immediately' may be a kind of apology – Shylock's hopeless attempt to play the father, but Jessica is no longer his daughter, and his farewell is a wretched cliché. This was consistently the most satisfying scene to play.

When Shylock arrives at the great scene of 3.1 Shakespeare has prepared the audience for his condition and has done half the actor's work for him with Solanio's description in 2.8 of his outrageous and uncontrolled passion at the loss of daughter and ducats. The intensity of this passion cannot be sustained and Shylock must be exhausted by his experience and very vulnerable. There is a plaintive, complaining tone about his first speeches and little threat in the repeated 'Let him look to his bond.' To Salerio's question 'Why, I am sure, if he forfeit, thou wilt not take his flesh. What's that good for?', Shylock can only impotently howl, 'To bait fish withal'. But from this cry of frustration grows Shylock's most famous speech. In rehearsals its reputation inhibited me. I stumbled unhappily through that quicksand of famous lines, memories of other actors' voices and rhythms in my head, and what proved to be a mistaken notion of what the speech was about: injustice, compassion, racial tolerance, equality and the evils of bad example. Interpreted this way the speech seemed to come from another play and had little connection with the Shylock of the earlier scenes. This reading, though fitting in parts, did not seem to be serving Shakespeare and made me very dissatisfied. At this point two things happened. I began to pay more attention to that word 'revenge', appearing in the speech like a recurring major chord. And I was lucky enough to see a paper by Professor Alan C. Dessen of the University of North Carolina which dealt with the very heart of the problem. Towards the end of his discussion of earlier plays about money-lenders, Dessen asks:

What then are we to conclude about the stage Jew as presented by Wilson, Marlowe, and Shakespeare? Although initially the three plays seem to have little in common, in each the same distinctive stage figure has served a comparable function – not merely to vilify Jews and Judaism but to challenge the professions of supposedly Christian London or Malta or Venice . . . By viewing Gerontus, Barabas, and Shylock as dramatic kinsmen, the modern reader can grasp the convention that stands behind them and informs them. In morality play, tragedy, or comedy, the stage Jew could function as a dramatic scalpel with which the Elizabethan dramatist could anatomize the inner reality of a society Christian in name but not necessarily in deed. The fact remains that Shakespeare *did* choose as his villain what seems to us an objectionable stereotype, but by recognizing the stage Jew as a potential theatrical device (and not a direct expression of authorial bigotry) we may be able to sidestep Shakespeare's alleged anti-semitism and instead appreciate the artistry with which he has incorporated such a stock figure into the world of romantic comedy.

(Alan C. Dessen, 'The Elizabethan Stage Jew',
Modern Language Quarterly 35 (1974), p. 244)

Here was the insight that transformed that speech from a muddled and sentimental bit of humanism to a vigorous justification of revenge by Christian example. And yet all this is only rhetoric, as Shylock has yet to hear the confirmation of Antonio's failure.

Tubal has not found Jessica in Genoa and in his grief and loss Shylock pitifully blurs the distinction between daughter and ducats, and wretchedly complains about the cost of searching for her. (At 'And I know not what's spent in the search', Tubal presented his bill of expenses which included, in writing just too small for the audience to read, a huge bar and restaurant bill for two nights at the Genoa Hilton.) Shylock becomes almost hysterical as he crashes from deep despair to wild elation at the alternating news of Jessica's profligacy and Antonio's losses, until he hears of the exchange of Leah's ring for a monkey. Here is something that cannot be priced, that 'a wilderness of monkeys' cannot equal, beyond value. A simple gift, possibly a betrothal ring, from a woman to her lover: 'I had it of Leah when I was a bachelor.' That word shatters our image of this man Shylock and we see the man that once was, a bachelor, with all the association of youth, innocence and love that is to come. Shakespeare doesn't need to write a pre-history of Shylock. Those two lines say it all. At this deepest moment of sorrow Tubal confirms that Antonio is utterly vulnerable, and *now* Shylock decides to kill him. No single incident or word is entirely responsible, but it is certainly Leah's ring and Shylock's confusion of love and grief that is the trigger. Shakespeare's choice of a name for Shylock's wife is interesting – John Russell Brown in the Arden Shakespeare points out that in Hebrew Leah means 'painful' or 'wearied'. Shylock and Tubal will meet at the synagogue and it is there that the 'oath in Heaven' will presumably be made. When we next see Shylock, the oath and the bond are public knowledge and, almost revelling in the general condemnation, Shylock chants and howls his murderous intention abroad. I felt there was a wildness about Shylock here, shown by the repetition of 'I'll have my bond', and the refusal to let Antonio speak, as if the anticipation of his deed has made him mad. This is the man that the unsuspecting Portia is preparing to meet.

Act 4, Scene 1 is often referred to as the trial scene or court scene. In fact it is neither. No one is on trial and there is no formal court – in the legal sense. It seems to be much closer to a hearing in chambers or a final, private appeal before the highest authority, the Duke. There is no judge and Portia is there as a legal expert, to advise the Duke and pronounce on law. Only those characters necessary to the action need be present. (In Charles Kean's production in the 1850s this scene had no fewer than twenty-six judges and forty senators.)

What a change there is in Shylock from the previous scene. He listens calmly without interruption to the Duke's speech, although it is not without provocation, and waits until he is invited to speak. In John Barton's production this mood of calm politeness and restraint was emphasized by the Duke himself serving Shylock with coffee. When at last he speaks, he is once more the controlled, articulate, witty man of 1.3. His words are almost apologetic at first, though quickly growing firmer. The speech becomes mockingly rhetorical, however, when he calls the cutting of Antonio's flesh a whim, and will not justify himself more than one would need over a troublesome rat, a gaping pig, a cat or a bagpipe. It's just a simple impulse, he says, like urinating. So this man is going to be killed, but his murder needed no justification, except, perhaps, that he is hated and loathed. Shylock is not going to waste this hour of triumph. The knife will be twisted many times before it enters Antonio's body, and everyone will suffer. Bassanio takes Shylock on, but is brushed aside like a troublesome fly. Antonio alone understands what Shylock is up to, and with fearless contempt towards him, he urges the sentence. Bassanio, judging others by himself, is still convinced that Shylock has his price, waves ducats in his face, and the Duke alludes to Shylock's prospects of mercy on judgement day; but this cannot frighten him and he again cites Christian example as his security. In this speech there is marvellous evidence of why Shylock is such a troubling character for an audience; deeply critical of society's cruelty, he uses a truly humanist argument to justify more wickedness. The speech returns to judgement at the end, but this time of the 'here and now' variety. The Duke threatens to dismiss the court and Shylock is alert at once. He will, of course, expect the Christians to trick him or slip out of their responsibility and he must watch their every move.

Shylock sharpening his knife is the black humorist at work again. Antonio is being stoical and noble, and Shylock's response is the crude reality of cold steel. It's just possible that it is also meant to frighten the young clerk (Nerissa). Gratiano thinks it will help to call Shylock an inexecrable dog and talk of his unhallowed dam, but Shylock politely refuses to be provoked. Instead he gives all his attention to Bellario's letter and the news of a 'young and learned doctor'. This could be the Christians' trick. Portia appears and Shylock becomes withdrawn and defensive. He gives nothing but his name and when again mercy is proposed Shylock tests this young doctor's quality with a simple 'Why?' Her answer is well known and it is a good speech, but I am convinced that what makes it remarkable in performance is that it is pure improvisation. Any interpretation that is at all predetermined will turn it into a tract. Portia proposes mercy because her upbringing and nature cannot conceive of any other response to someone in such difficulty. She has never imagined that anyone could ask 'why mercy?' or that such a person could exist. She is invited to justify something which is as natural to her as breathing and it is the shock of that which motivates 'The quality of mercy is not strained', and we are moved as we hear her articulate her faith, perhaps for the first time. I believe that Shylock too is moved by her words and that is why he has to dredge up the terrible oath, 'My deeds upon my head'. Bassanio is still offering more money (Portia's presumably) and bits of himself he is never likely to have to pay; but when he begs the Duke to twist the law, 'to do a great right, do a little wrong', we see the real slippery opportunist at work. This is what Shylock has been expecting, though perhaps not quite so crudely proposed. Portia's response, therefore, is utterly unexpected. Suddenly she is standing by his side supporting him. The Venetians' legal lackey turns out to be honest. Shylock is euphoric and for the first time in the scene he loses control. He stops thinking, watching and listening and his defences drop. Had he continued to think he would have known this 'honest' person would not let him take a man's life. Had he truly listened he would have heard her continue to urge mercy as before, and had he watched her face, he would have seen her struggling to save him from the blows that are to come. She even allows Shylock a glimpse of her trump card – the blood clause – by indicating that Antonio may bleed to death; but at last she hardens her heart against Shylock when he refuses to provide a surgeon to stop Antonio's wounds. Shylock has set himself up and the thunderbolts are about to fall.

Bassanio and Gratiano would see their wives dead if it could save Antonio's life. Hollow words again, but interesting for Portia and Nerissa to hear. The sentence is given and Shylock moves in to carry it out and the trap closes. In the past I had been puzzled by the speed at which Shylock slams into reverse, from 'A sentence, come prepare' to 'I take this offer then.' If the interpretation is heroic or sentimental I don't know how the actor does it. If it's pragmatic, then it's easy. Shylock is told he will lose his

2 'Thy eyes shall be thy judge'

26

lands and his goods. Portia plays the blood card. Shylock immediately sees the (expected) trap he has walked into, considers for a moment that he will lose, checks the law, and knows at once that he must back off. What is delightful about Shylock at this moment is that, though under threat, he still tries to make off with three times the value of the bond. Portia is stubborn and Shylock, not really understanding her, and thinking himself back in the market place, tries to bargain with her. He will settle for his principal. Now, however, the experienced survivor begins to smell real danger and he knows he must put distance between himself and this place; but the ground is opening up beneath him and when the word 'alien' hits his ears he knows he is to be finished off. Once again he is an outsider, without rights and utterly vulnerable. This is no place for pride or heroics. Shylock knows if he wants to survive he must get down in the dirt and grovel. So his life is spared. He howls and whines and he gets back half his fortune. They want him to become a Christian and bequeath his estate to Lorenzo and Jessica and he is content because he has saved something when moments before he had nothing. Now he must get away before they change their minds or think up further punishment. Illness is a good excuse and he leaves them with the assurance that the deed *will* be signed.

Every actor playing Shylock looks for an effective way to 'get off'. Kean apparently went through a startling physical change on his exit. Edwin Booth invented an elaborate and melodramatic mime. Irving was still and tragically defeated, letting out a long sigh as he left; and recently, Laurence Olivier left his effect for offstage when, after a moment of silence, the audience heard a despairing howl of grief and rage. Here Gratiano provided the clue. He makes a cruel joke out of Shylock's christening, and the person who must laugh most is, of course, Shylock. And so he leaves. It saddened me that people were upset by the squalor of Shylock's ending, rather than angry that it should be necessary and moved by the tragedy of 'You take my life / When you do take the means whereby I live', and the humiliation of 'I am content.' Shylock is a great role and in its way a tragic one. Its power over actors and audiences alike may be in part because he is not a king or tyrant or great lover, but a small, complex, real and recognizable human being, part of us all. The role took me by surprise and I learned again the important lesson on the foolishness of coming to Shakespeare with preconceived ideas. Everything I once felt about the part was turned upside down and where there had been indifference I became a passionate enthusiast. I know that I was lucky, too. This was a perfect instance of that rare and blessed identification with a character, which an actor cannot manufacture, but which will, at the most unexpected moment, pounce, grab him by the throat and invade his heart. It is said that an actor must love the character he plays – however unpleasant. I loved Shylock and know that it was a privilege to be given an insight into such a life.

Portia in
The Merchant of Venice
SINEAD CUSACK

SINEAD CUSACK began acting at an early age, playing juvenile leads with the Abbey Theatre in Dublin before gaining repertory experience in England. After a Juliet in London, a Desdemona at Ludlow, a Raina at the Oxford Festival and on tour, and appearances in a wide range of parts in films and television, she joined the Royal Shakespeare Company in 1979. Her work for the Company, in the two Stratford theatres, in Newcastle and in London, includes Grace Harkaway in *London Assurance*, Lady Amaranth in *Wild Oats* and Evadne in *The Maid's Tragedy*, besides Isabella in *Measure for Measure*, Katherine in *The Taming of the Shrew* and Beatrice in *Much Ado About Nothing*. In 1980, she won the Clarence Derwent Award for Best Supporting Actress for her performance as Celia in *As You Like It*. In 1981, she appeared as Portia in *The Merchant of Venice*, with David Suchet as Shylock, in a production designed by Christopher Morley and directed by John Barton.

I failed when I played Portia. By which I mean that when I do it again – if I do – I'll do it differently. Let me say a little about the history of Portia and myself. I read *The Merchant of Venice* for the first time, as most of us probably did, at about the age of fourteen, and I delighted in it. Although I had read quite a few of the plays at that time – my father being an actor, and ours being a very theatrical household – it was Portia who captured my imagination more than any other Shakespearean character. I liked what I saw in her on that first reading – warmth and humanity, together with wit and a shining intelligence. I have since, over the years, seen maybe three or four productions, and I have to say that on all occasions I left the theatre not liking Portia very much, and I couldn't understand why. I finally worked out that the great problem for the actress playing the role is to reconcile the girl at home in Belmont early in the play with the one who plays a Daniel come to judgement in the Venetian court. I couldn't understand why

Shakespeare makes her so unsympathetic in those early scenes – the spoilt little rich girl dismissing suitor after suitor in very witty and derisory fashion. The girl who does that, I thought, is not the woman to deliver the 'quality of mercy' speech. I knew that was a problem.

Although all my life I had wanted, more than any other part, to play Portia, when I was finally asked to do so, by John Barton, in December 1980, I said no. I look back astounded at the arrogance of that reaction, but at the time it seemed right and proper. John had already done a small-theatre production at The Other Place in 1978 and had transferred it to the Warehouse in the season following. The production had had two Portias – Marjorie Bland in Stratford and Lisa Harrow in London. I had not seen it, but I thought John's ideas would probably be very fully formed, and that I might be straitjacketed into a performance not my own. The role would have been worked out with other players, and I feared I would not be allowed to grow into it in my own way. On two previous occasions I had taken over roles from other actresses and the experience had left me jaundiced. I said no, and it was a distressing moment of my life. However, it took a couple of dinners out, we discussed it, and John persuaded me.

I remember a professional tip that my father once gave me – 'Always look for the comedy in tragedy, and for the tragedy in comedy.' I set out to find a distinctly tragic Portia, and I was glad to learn that John was ready to encourage me. It turned out that, while we differed here and there about the play, our ideas about Portia were very close. He also saw her as a passionate, human and loving girl, and, unlike many directors, he took her to be the centre of the play. Our biggest area of disagreement as we talked about the play concerned its last scene, which I like to think of as yet another trial scene. Bassanio is on trial when he makes choice of the caskets, Shylock is on trial in the court scene, and Bassanio on trial again when he returns to Belmont after betraying a trust. The final scene, I argued, should not be played as a mischievous little game; it was not comic. John in his wisdom said, 'You can combine the two, Sinead. There is room for the important issues of love and the betrayal of love within a comedic framework.' And so we agreed, and moved on to other topics.

I was, of course, eager to know the rest of the cast, and the first question that comes to every Portia's mind is 'Who is playing Shylock?' It is strange, for Portia and Shylock have only one scene together while she and Bassanio have many. I was delighted to hear that it was David Suchet, for he is a consummate actor and I love playing with him. Portia's relationship with Shylock is brief but it forms the climax of the play and I looked forward to

3   'If you do love me, you will find me out'
Sinead Cusack as Portia, April 1981

working it out with David, who was also coming new to the production. Rehearsals started in January.

All directors have their different systems of working, and John's is extraordinary in that he does not believe in the preliminary 'read-through' and he does believe in the 'solo-call'. The cast never assemble to discuss the play as a whole, and they are likely to be called on to rehearse separately, in isolation from the scene and from most of, or all of, the other players. Sometimes you find this useful, because you are not intimidated by other actors, don't have to give them something, and feel more free to explore the part. On the other hand, it can make you form ideas in a vacuum, and when the time comes to respond to your fellow actors you find you are not doing it at all. I think this a drawback in John's rehearsal process. He does tend to isolate his actors from one another – an effect very apparent in his production of *Hamlet*. I don't like the system, and both David Suchet and I fought against it very strongly. However, I had enjoyed the unusual privilege of talking with the director about the nature of the play, and in practice we rehearsed many scenes in pairs, the first call being upon Corrina Seddon and myself, with an invitation to look through all the Portia/Nerissa scenes in the play.

We sat around a table, over endless cups of coffee and cigarettes, and discussed our impressions of that immensely important first scene in Belmont. We felt that if we got that scene right for Portia, everything else would follow. We concentrated first on her youth, for it seemed to me that she is, at the beginning of the play, very young. She moves from despair to laughter, from anger to filial obedience, and I found myself likening her mercurial moods to those of my nineteen-year-old sister. John saw Nerissa as the older and more worldly of the two, loving Portia, but forever cheering her up, joking with her and reasoning with her. Corinna (six years younger than I am) felt that the age-difference was unimportant and was content to concentrate on the friendship, but John insisted on Nerissa's sophistication and dressed her in bright pink in his production, which otherwise presented a sombre Belmont.

John's idea was to set the scene in autumnal gloom, with Portia seated on a bench contemplating the caskets in a mood of despair and misery when Nerissa enters. I liked the idea of carrying the caskets around with me wherever I went, to remind me of my horrible dilemma. Portia is bound by a promise given to her father on his deathbed to abide by his will, and to marry only the man who chooses the correct casket. She chafes against the restriction that curbs 'the will of a living daughter' by 'the will of a dead father'. Yet she is adamant in her resolve to honour her father's conditions. When Nerissa tentatively suggests to her that she might be won 'by some other sort than your father's imposition', Portia responds uncompromisingly, 'If I live to be as old as Sibylla, I will die as chaste as Diana, unless I be obtained by the manner of my father's will.' Taking her predicament seriously, I decided to play Portia's words 'my little body is aweary of this great world', not in the bored voice of a child who has too much of everything, but as a cry of anguish from one who finds the whole business of the caskets very painful. But I did not feel that Portia submits merely from filial obedience. There is something in her nature that is attracted by the idea of 'a test'. Marriage is not to be embarked on easily and thoughtlessly, and that, I thought, is why Bassanio's betrayal of her later in the play will cause her such distress.

Portia's mood switches from one extreme to another as she takes comfort from Nerissa's reassurances about her father's lottery – 'holy men at their death have good inspirations', and accepts the suggestion that they run through the list of suitors. We agreed that at this point Nerissa may well be prompting Portia to laugh in spite of her tears. I liked this idea very much and worked hard at it. But it is a difficult moment for the players of both Portia and Nerissa. For Nerissa the problem is to give colour and shape to that interminable list, and for Portia it is to escape the effect of a spoilt brat maliciously destroying her suitors. Both in rehearsal and in performance this scene caused me more trouble than any other. I think we finally made it work, although it was at the price of cutting out the Scotsman, and perhaps one or two others.

We decided early in rehearsal that neither Portia nor Nerissa knew the contents of the caskets, and that Portia's suggestion that Nerissa set a glass of Rhenish wine 'on the contrary casket' was no more than an inconsequential joke. We also decided that no suitor had yet undergone the ritual of choice. Both decisions made good theatrical sense, heightening the tensions of expectation and highlighting the horror of both Portia's predicament and that of her unfortunate wooers (under oath 'never to woo a lady afterward in way of marriage').

From John's original production at The Other Place I inherited an old raincoat. When he first revived the idea I said, 'I don't want a raincoat', and he said, 'I think that Portia misses her father so much she wears his coat.' Indeed he lent me his bearskin and I used to love playing in John's mouldy old coat (you discovered the most revolting things in his pocket). I was pleased by the idea that Portia didn't care how she looked. It fitted well with my conviction that she is unschooled in the social ways of men and the world, and awkward in her relationship with Bassanio. That shabby raincoat related Portia to the distant world of her father, the wise and 'ever virtuous' old man who understood the law and money and marriage. She has no idea of her own attractiveness, her own appeal. At Belmont she lives in a woman's world, and John accentuated the idea by casting Balthazar, one of her manservants, as a woman – we called her Betty Balthazar. John gave no reason (he never gives reasons) but I suppose he liked the idea of three girls in the household with no men, leaving them tender and vulnerable, with all those suitors coming at them.

We played the suitor scenes for their grim, rather than their comic, qualities. I sat in a chair with the caskets in front of me, Nerissa and Betty on either side, while Morocco and Arragon circled us like animals getting ready to pounce, one might say, upon their pound of flesh. Again, this way of playing the scene underscored the pathos of Portia's predicament ('I stand for sacrifice', as she puts it later to Bassanio) and her courage in abiding by her father's harsh dictates. Yet this effect may be a little at odds with her interest in, and perhaps her confidence in, the 'good inspiration' of the lottery test.

John had me roped as part of the ritual. One day at rehearsal he said to me 'Sinead, I had a great idea in my bath. What about your being tied up?' Obviously he had seen *The Maid's Tragedy* in which I played the king's mistress and tied him up before killing him. I fought against my bondage for a while, but he was wedded to the idea and roped I was. (Unknown to John, I managed to lose the rope somewhere between Stratford and London.) The rope was made of silver, gold and lead, and placed ritualistically over my lap – I wasn't actually tied up. It was meant to highlight the idea that I was a sort of sacrificial victim. And yet I had to keep my confidence in my father and in the test he had devised. Much depended, therefore, on my expectations of Bassanio. For, while Shylock's role is important for Portia, Bassanio's is much more so. In early rehearsals we spent a lot of time speculating on the relationship between Portia and Bassanio before the play begins. Bassanio talks to Antonio of the fair speechless messages he received from her when he formerly visited Belmont, and Portia in her first scene with Nerissa recalled Bassanio the 'scholar and soldier' who came to Belmont in the company of the Marquis of Montferrat. The discussion was never really resolved, but I felt sure that, however brief and mute their meeting, the effect on Portia had been overwhelming. I therefore played the first mention of him, not as a vague and distant recollection, but as a poignant memory of one I had loved, in however young and adolescent a fashion, from the first moment I had set eyes on him.

For Jonathan Hyde, playing Bassanio, the choice was much more difficult. He speaks of her as

> a lady richly left,
> And she is fair and, fairer than that word,
> Of wondrous virtues. (1.1.161–3)

The precedence given to the riches made such an impression that Jonathan (and John Barton) decided that Bassanio in his first scene with Portia should concentrate on making the right choice of casket rather than on wooing the lady. This produced some memorable moments in rehearsal – Jonathan circling the caskets while I followed him around and addressed the whole of the 'I pray you tarry' speech to his retreating back. On one occasion, at the end of that speech Jonathan turned and said 'Sinead, what were you saying just now?' I explained that I was painfully telling him that I loved him and that I couldn't bear the idea of his going through the ritual in case he made the wrong choice. He nodded, thanked me, and said he thought he ought to start listening to the speech in future and maybe 'looking at you now and again'. Until then he had seemed unaware of my presence.

Now, in retrospect, I see that I approached both the first and the climactic scenes with Bassanio in the wrong spirit. In my early days of playing Shakespeare I never smiled. My Desdemona was dour and my Juliet joyless. I learnt to smile and laugh in Shakespeare only when I played Celia in *As You Like It*, realizing that the delight and fun of comedy were of a piece with its seriousness. I forgot this, for me, momentous discovery, when I performed the 'I pray you tarry' speech for its desperation and not its love. Now I see that there is pain in it, but that her protest against the restraint imposed on her by her father's will is overlaid with a playful and affectionate awareness that her own distress must not be pressed upon Bassanio. The punctuation of the speech shows how hard she is trying not to say too much:

> One half of me is yours, the other half yours –
> Mine own, I would say. (3.2.16–17)

She stops, she starts, she says one thing and contradicts herself with another. She begins by saying merely that the wrong choice on his part will deprive her of his company, but she ends by proclaiming

35

herself all Bassanio's and to hell with the consequences. I didn't get that mixture of humour and despair right for many months, merely because I stupidly thought that declarations of love should always be worthy and earnest, untouched with comedy and an awareness of one's own idiocy.

The staging of the scene's first movement altered from day to day, and was not satisfactorily resolved until we took the play to London. But the staging of Bassanio's choice and of Portia's response was decided early in rehearsal. John wanted Portia isolated centre-stage, under a spotlight, from the moment when she bids 'Nerissa and the rest stand all aloof.' Bassanio was to circle about her in the shadows throughout her speech likening him to Hercules and herself to 'the tribute paid by howling Troy to the sea monster'. At the end of this magnificent speech (again with its touch of comedy and wry objectivity – 'with much, much more dismay / I view the fight than thou that mak'st the fray') comes the song.

Now, the text does not specify the singer of the song. Traditionally it is given to Nerissa or to a special singer for the occasion but John was determined, stubborn, obdurate and intractable – that Portia should sing it. His reason was valid: Portia is telling Bassanio that appearance is not everything. But my reaction as an actress was horror. I cannot sing and the idea of singing after such a long and difficult speech appalled me (the more so, perhaps, because Jonathan Hyde is married to a great opera singer). I felt that a musical number would be out of keeping, but John insisted that Portia was dredging up the song from childhood memories and found it apt for that occasion. I have to admit that after playing it for so long and listening to audience reactions I have come to agree. I still find it hard to do and my voice cracks on the top note, but I think the effect wonderfully theatrical; and it also makes sense that Portia should use every means at her disposal, without dishonouring her oath, to point Bassanio in the right direction. Early in rehearsal I discounted, as too cheap or trite on either Shakespeare's or Portia's part, the idea that the three rhymes ('bread', 'head', 'nourishèd') invited the fourth rhyme 'lead'. The wonder of that moment of choice hits me anew every time I play it. Portia cries to love to moderate and allay her ecstasy, remembers all she had had to endure in obedience to her father's will – 'As doubtful thoughts, and rash embraced despair' (3.2.109–10) – and bids them all a glad farewell. She breaks out of the terrible prison her father's love has built for her. Every time I speak that speech I salute Portia's courage and endurance, and it is these qualities that she later takes into the courtroom in Venice.

Bassanio looks to Portia for her signature and ratification of his choice and at this point we took a little licence, not with the text perhaps but with its performance. I look from Bassanio to the caskets and then in joyful abandon I pick up those wretched boxes, which have threatened me for so long, and I fling them violently across the room. Again, it is an unashamedly theatrical moment, but it serves as a release of tension both for the audience and for the actress playing Portia. It provides too a springboard for the speech 'You see me, Lord Bassanio, where I stand' which has as much to do with release as with commitment. Her commitment nevertheless is total and passionate. He takes the ring in the same spirit and vows that only death will part him from it. At this point Venice casts its grim shadow over magical Belmont, as Bassanio receives news of Antonio's predicament. Portia, liberated and married, has come of age and is ready now to move in a larger world.

I like to think that both Bassanio and Portia grow wiser and more mature in the course of the play, and particularly in the casket 'trial'. Bassanio begins as a feckless ne'er-do-well and opportunist but it must be love of Portia that moves him to make the right choice. Jonathan found it hard to believe that he fell in love with Portia in the course of making his choice, and preferred to think that they had been together for some weeks. However, my speech 'I pray you tarry' made that impossible. Bassanio has to rise to the occasion to pass the test, to win both Portia and the gold by making the humble choice of lead. The choice is liberating for them both, for by making it he proves his worth.

Owing to John's way of working and rehearsing, however, Bassanio's relationship with Antonio in Venice was kept from me until a very late stage in rehearsal. David Suchet and I had worked in isolation through the courtroom scene, but when the time came to put it all together we were in for some surprises. We had been directed to look at each other, but out of the corners of our eyes we noticed that there was an undressing process going on downstage right, between Antonio and Bassanio, which was riveting in its detail. Collar studs and buttons were being undone, all in mime of course, and there was a lot of kissing. Finally David (I didn't have the courage) asked what was going on. Tom Wilkinson playing Antonio said 'I am getting ready for the moment when I bare my chest.' When David protested 'This is the focus of the scene, not that', Tom said 'Well, look, you have got all the text.' It is true that to distract focus on stage you do not have to say anything. There is a famous story about the Lunts. She had a great soliloquy to deliver down front, and he was upstage, sitting

4   'Art thou contented, Jew?'

behind a table, smoking a cigarette. About half way through her soliloquy she noticed that the whole focus of attention had shifted from her to her husband. She thought 'What's he doing?' and turned and looked, but he was sitting there, no movement at all, just smoking. The audience had left her entirely and she finished up very lamely. That went on for three nights – she would check him, and he was doing nothing. She finally discovered he had put a hair-grip through his cigarette so that his ash didn't drop off. So it was with Antonio and Bassanio downstage – we didn't have a chance. We did compromise in the end, but Antonio continued to undress a lot, and the *Sunday Times* critic, James Fenton, spent a lot of space on the matter. In spite of the setback I felt that David and I found a convincing way of playing the courtroom scene. The nature of the rehearsals encouraged the two of us to form a very strong theatrical relationship that excluded the rest of the world and the court. Shylock and Portia are head and shoulders above the rest of the group and are fighting a battle there, just the two of them. I decided that when I entered the courtroom I knew exactly how to save Antonio; my cousin had shown me that loophole in the law which would save him from his bond. A lot of people ask why then does Portia put everyone through all that misery and why does she play cat-and-mouse with Shylock. The reason is that she doesn't go into the courtroom to save Antonio (that's easy) but to save Shylock, to redeem him – she is passionate to do that. She gives him opportunity after opportunity to relent and to exercise his humanity. She proposes mercy and charity but he still craves the law. She offers him thrice his money but he sticks to his oath. It is only when he shows himself totally ruthless and intractable (refusing even to allow a surgeon to stand by) that she offers him more justice than he desires.

I was satisfied with the Portia/Shylock relationship and I think David was too. But the courtroom scene also initiates the ring-play which is so important in the last act. When Bassanio tells Antonio that he is married to a wife 'as dear to him as life itself' and that he 'would sacrifice wife, life, and world to save him', Shakespeare gives Portia one of her big laugh-lines: 'Your wife would give you little thanks for that.' I found the laugh difficult to accept (although I had to accept it) because I believed that Bassanio's willingness to part with the ring must have been very hurtful to Portia. Now I begin to change my mind. From the start I took the last scene to be another painful trial scene and I tried to play it that way. Now I see more clearly that it is, after all, Portia herself who wins the ring back from Bassanio. She wins both ways, and is in a wonderful position to know the whole truth about Bassanio in the courtroom, and is therefore in a position to show him something as well as to forgive him.

There is a big difference too between life in Venice and life in Belmont, to which we return at the end of the play, but this wasn't always made clear in the production. John made it rather a gloomy place, and not very far away in mood and style from Venice. Perhaps because the production began in The Other Place, the cast was very small, and I should have been glad of more people about in Venice, particularly in the courtroom. There should be something fabulous about Belmont where 'patines of bright gold' and 'the sweet power of music' can change our nature, if only 'for a time'. Some details of costume and design didn't help either. Jonathan Hyde, for example, persuaded the designer Christopher Morley to make a swinging Byronic cloak for Bassanio in Venice; but there is no justification whatever for him turning up at Portia's in the same coat – what did he do with the three thousand ducats he got to furnish him for Belmont?

If I return to the play I shall give fresh thought to Portia and Bassanio. Perhaps she changes him. She gives him the ring, wins it back from him, and gives it to him again. She teaches him 'doubly to see himself'. Perhaps I wasn't quite witty enough, nor sure or light enough in touch in these last scenes – and that is why I failed when I played Portia.

Malvolio in
Twelfth Night

DONALD SINDEN

ONALD SINDEN, an Associate Artist of the Royal Shakespeare Company, first appeared at Stratford in 1946. After taking leading parts in London in many classic and modern plays, as well as establishing a reputation through films and television, he returned to Stratford in 1963 to play Richard Plantagenet in the *Wars of the Roses*. His work for the Royal Shakespeare Company gives further proof of his versatility: his range covers Henry VIII, Benedick, King Lear and Othello. His Malvolio was first given at Stratford in 1969. This production, designed by Christopher Morley and including Judi Dench as Viola, Bill Fraser as Sir Toby Belch and Emrys James as Feste, was directed by John Barton. Donald Sinden published the first volume of his autobiography, *A Touch of the Memoirs*, in 1982; a second volume (*Laughter in the Second Act*) is appearing in March 1985.

Why is it so difficult to record in words a theatrical performance? Critics such as Hazlitt, Coleridge, Agate and Tynan have given us their own responses to certain performances; and we have some heavily annotated scripts of actors and actresses such as Sarah Siddons and Ellen Terry. But I cannot recall an attempt by an actor to analyse his own performance, to set down what he thought and did, what he tried to achieve, where and how he succeeded, move by move. That is what I am attempting here. Not that I think my interpretation of Malvolio in 1970 was definitive – no Shakespearean performance ever is. I do think it fitted John Barton's conception of *Twelfth Night*, however, and it was well received by the public.

I first saw *Twelfth Night* at Stratford-upon-Avon in 1947, and in the following year appeared as Sebastian in the Old Vic production directed by Sir Alec Guinness. I fully appreciated the charm of this delightful play, so much so that when early in 1969 John Barton telephoned to ask me to play Malvolio I unhesitatingly said 'yes'. It was to be the penultimate produc-

5   'My Lady calls'
Donald Sinden as Malvolio, August 1969

tion of the season, to be followed by *Henry VIII* in which I was to play the King. Rehearsals were begun two days after I left my current play *Not Now Darling*. When I reread *Twelfth Night*, however, I soon realized that this was not the play I thought I knew. Troubled, I telephoned John Barton : 'I am afraid you may have to recast Malvolio – I find him tragic.' 'Thank God for that', he replied, 'I thought I would have to talk you round to it.' I was committed. Before rehearsals started I read the play some ten times. Slowly, oh so slowly I hammer myself into the character until by the time of the first performance I can step in and out of his shoes. I look for any character-building phrase in the script, and try to analyse his attitudes to circumstances both in the play and out of it. Though I have read most books on the theory of acting, I subscribe to no one method but try to judge performances by a tenet of Ellen Terry's: 'To act you must make the thing written your own; you must steal the words, steal the thoughts, and convey the stolen treasure to others with great art.'

What kind of man is Malvolio? What is his background? I see him as a military man; unpopular at school, he joins the army and, while he displays no quality of leadership, he is so damned efficient that he now finds himself, at forty-five, a Colonel in the Pay Corps, embittered, with no prospect of further promotion. He has bored every woman he has met and he stays unmarried. A certain widowed Count I suppose needed a major-domo to manage his Mediterranean estate, and who better than this totally efficient and honest teetotaller? When Malvolio arrives in Illyria he is shocked by its *asolare* mood and its spongeing layabouts. There is Sir Toby (perhaps the English brother of the dead Countess), but there is nothing easier to manage than a drunk; then the Fool, whose tasteless jokes fail to amuse Malvolio, who goes Absent Without Leave, and must be disciplined; and Maria (aged fifty in Barton's production and sometime governess to the Count's daughter) could be brought to heel if only she wouldn't consort with people above her station. As for the suitors, Aguecheek, that eccentric fifty-year-old Scot (Barton's version), and the arty Count Orsino – but I am already thinking as Malvolio!

As I rehearse, the muscles of my face and my whole body begin to react to the tensions within Malvolio. The military years have left their mark: an erect stance, nearly always at 'Attention', and when 'At Ease' never fully relaxed. Originally I had wanted to carry a short cane, but being persuaded that it would evoke quite the wrong period I settled for the long staff of office, but always felt that to Malvolio it was an encumbrance. He has a small, tight, mean mouth, the corners of which turn down. The inner ends of his eyebrows are elevated and the outer pulled down in an expression of permanent supercilious scorn for his minions. He is thin – too thin – from his years of austerity. Now, I as an actor am not thin enough! Yet the actor in the comedy must tell the audience as much as he can at his first entrance. What can make-up and costume do for me? I spend a great deal of time observing my fellow creatures, trying to find 'copy' for the character I play, and frequently I find my 'face' in an art gallery. On this occasion I visited the Tate and found my Malvolio in Graham Sutherland's splendid elongated portrait of Somerset Maugham. The eyebrows, the mouth, the wrinkles – every one of them vertical, and that is what I must be: vertical – the knees close together, the hair very thin on top but grown long in an attempt to cover the balding pate, above all the colour – yellow, jaundiced. I take a postcard; I have my make-up.

Now for the costume. The designer has placed the setting for this production at about the year 1603. Late Elizabethan, early Jacobean. The costume designer and I agree that Malvolio should be dressed in black: high-heeled shoes (adding height), black stockings (slimming), breeches, doublet (very tight), and the black only relieved by very narrow, plain, white collar and cuffs. I choose a period hat like a black flower pot (height again and vertical line), and an overcoat with a large raised collar which in silhouette continues the line from hat-to-shoulders-to-hip. Malvolio must have a chain of office (a thin one with a large circular disc). This could run across the chest, but no – better run it round the neck and down as near vertical as possible. Somerset Maugham's hair would be quite out of period so we make a wig with long straight hair faintly curled at the bottom all round the head, with a few strands to cover the dome, now padded to give an egg-like look. All this was not thought up in advance, of course, but day by day as rehearsals were under way.

In performance the character must move in specific stage conditions, in this instance on a permanent set designed by Christopher Morley. It represented a long room or gallery running away from the audience in deep perspective, with double doors at the far end and entrance Downstage Left and Right. I have always thought that a stage should be mapped out on graph paper so that a prompt-script could denote somewhat more precise positions. As it is we merely write, for example, 'X D R' which assumes the knowledge (previously recorded) that we were formerly 'U C'. Quite often one will shift weight from one foot to the other; while this can change emphasis it is very rarely recorded. In the account that follows I have used this simplified convention but have added one of my own. Laughs are not

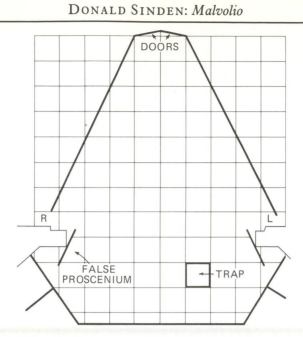

6*a*   Plan of stage for John Barton's production of *Twelfth Night*, 1969

6*b*   Set designed by Christopher Morley for *Twelfth Night* (Act 1, Scene 2), 1969

normally recorded, but the comic actor is always striving for them, and I would like to be able to rate their size from 1–9, between the largest that can be expected (9) and the smallest (1) still worth trying for.

'If music be the food of love' – the play has started, and I shall try to give you my thoughts and Malvolio's, objective and subjective, at key points of its performance.

Before the start of Act 1, Scene 3 the Olivia household is returning from church; entering Left and straight to the centre of the stage, a sharp Right turn, Up and out of the door U C leaving Toby behind with his first line. As I move toward the centre carrying my staff I look to my left – people! What are they doing there? (Laugh 3.) Again leading a procession in Scene 5, but no coat and hat, I enter this time R. I glower at Feste, for I have persuaded Olivia that he must go and she has promised to dismiss him; I assist Olivia to her chair D R. None of this is exaggerated and only a tiny fraction of the audience notices it. Fabian and another servant are in attendance slightly Upstage C. Fabian has a drink on a tray which he hands me and which I proffer to Olivia; she doesn't want it so I return it to Fabian, take a book from him and give it to Olivia, glance at its cover and see it is not at all suitable. 'Take the Fool away', says Olivia. If only she wouldn't personally give orders to the servants. She ought to do it through me. But with a quick jerk of my staff to them I think I can make it appear that that was the original intention. But what is the Fool saying? 'Take away the *Lady*.' Good God, he should be shot. What a bore he is, but she gives in to him and I walk L and turn my back to the populace, who again seem to have gathered. 'What think you of this Fool, Malvolio? doth he not mend?' Wham! Right into my court and in front of all these people. What can I say? The most grudging, sour, nasal 'Nyeas' (laugh 4). The actor needs a laugh there, as his next line is vicious, 'and shall do till the pangs of death shake him'. Feste answers with a feeble joke at which Maria dares to laugh – a glower, a rap on the floor and a jerk of my staff and she is sent scurrying. 'How say you to that, Malvolio?' From a great height and with positive delight I can reply 'he is out of his guard already, unless you laugh' (pronounced as one might say 'vomit'). Then, with a look across the theatre circle, 'I take these wise men that crow so . . . no better than the fool's zanies.' Did I see a smile on Fabian's face? 'I'll have his guts for garters.' I am now one-hundred-per-cent Malvolio, but in a comedy I, the actor, must remain one-hundred-per-cent myself, standing outside my character, my ears out on stalks listening for the very slightest sound from the audience, controlling them, so that I am able to steer a 'cue', 'punch' or 'tag' line clear of any interruption. If on any night Malvolio takes over, the precision, the immaculate timing, the control suffer. If the actor takes over, the performance becomes 'technical' and the audience is always aware of it. (This last is often a fault of mine and my wife lets me know it.)

Malvolio's next entrance shows him at a loss, foot faulted, off-guard, vulnerable, outfaced by a mere chit of a boy. Ostensibly to ask for further instructions I enter from L rapidly, the staff now out of control, and on arriving C my mouth opens – but to say what? My finger tips to my lips (does he bite his nails?) and Olivia is looking at me waiting. I must try to say something, pull myself together: 'Madam' (pronounced Mairdom; laugh 3), producing it from a stutter of B's D's T's and P's to make the word much more incongruous. I finish in desperation, 'What is to be said to him, Lady? – he's fortified against *any* denial.' She answers, 'Tell him he shall not speak with me.' This solution seems never to have occurred to me. With a civil inclination I start off quickly L but after four steps I am caught in mid-air and turn towards Olivia, for I had quite forgotten. 'H'as been told so' (laugh 3). 'What kind of man is he?' What an extraordinary question! 'Why, of *mankind*' (laugh 1). 'What manner of man', 'Of very *ill* manner' (laugh 2). I look off L. Then Olivia, as to a child, 'Of what personage and years is he?' A great light dawns – at last I see what she is getting at. Here I interpose 'Ahhh!' (laugh 2), and speak grudgingly on. But Olivia answers, 'Let him approach.' I must obey; I turn and begin to exit quickly L but I am again caught in mid-air by 'Call in my gentlewoman!' Oh dear! One thing at a time, please. A sharp about turn and my staff is Jove-like banged on the floor and the voice that roars 'Gentlewoman' is of the parade-ground (laugh 4). Maria comes scuttling on from R. 'May Lady calls', I explain, with the implication that the voice that thundered 'Gentlewoman' was Olivia's (laugh 4). With scornful dignity and elegant use of my staff, I exit L. No sooner out of 'the presence' I am faced with that maddening Cesario again. As I return to announce 'him', before I can utter a word, I am shaken to discover that Olivia and Maria have both lowered their veils.

As Cesario is shortly to play upon this point, I must not as an actor forestall it; however, as Malvolio, I cannot allow it to go unnoticed; my reaction is therefore infinitesimal.

While I am still undetermined about whom I should speak to, Cesario enters and says to Olivia: 'The honourable lady of the house, which is she?' Can I believe what I hear? This chit of a boy takes incredible liberties, and suddenly Olivia says: 'Give us the place alone.' Leave a young man and young girl alone! But that is an order, so a rap with my staff and pointing it R, I indicate that Maria must leave – and before me. She does so and I look Cesario over from head to foot and slowly, very slowly; with efficient use of my staff exit R.

Every night at this point I would wait in the wings for my next entrance – partly because I personally enjoyed listening to the enchanting scene between Cesario and Olivia and partly because I felt that Malvolio would do precisely the same – his ear glued to the keyhole. 'What ho, Malvolio!' His military reflex action is to reply: 'Here, Madam', patently betraying the fact that he is, to say the least, lurking (laugh 2). I came into view from the R entrance and under cover of a laugh from the audience I made my way to C. Malvolio recovers dignity *en route* – his attention riveted on the 'door' L through which Cesario has just left. He is hardly aware that he then adds: 'At your service.' Olivia begins: 'Run after that same . . .' This is *too* much! Never in my life – at least not for many years have I been *ordered* to do anything so indecorous; shocked, shattered, I echo: 'Run?!' (laugh 8). John Barton always disapproved of this. He did not mind my reaction or that I should *mouth* 'Run', but I was not to vocalize it. The difference for me was between a titter and a theatre-shaking belly laugh. We finally agreed, 'Matinées only'. Subsequently in Australia Trevor Nunn found himself having to rehearse some replacements to the cast – John Barton being detained in Stratford-upon-Avon. When we came to this scene he asked me why I no longer got a laugh at this point of the play. I explained that John Barton had said that my 'run' was not in the text. 'Ah; but', said Nunn equivocally, 'it *is* in the subtext.' So back it went for the rest of the tour! Malvolio only half hears the rest of her instructions and is not quite sure when she has finished. She gives him the ring which he has to almost force on to his much larger finger while couching the staff in the crook of his elbow. A pause, then she adds: 'Hie thee, Malvolio.' I am deeply hurt that she should speak thus to me – but what am I to do? Pained and distressed I reply: 'Madam' (I'm sorry you should behave like this) 'I will.' I turn L, the staff is held by its centre, horizontally, in the right hand and I execute what must be the slowest run ever (one critic called it 'a Zulu lope'), as if crossing a series of puddles just wider than an extended pace. I exit L (laugh 8, and round of applause).

John Barton here transposed Act 2, Scenes 1 and 2. The chair and sunshade were replaced by a long bench, the door U C opened and we are in a street. Cesario enter Upstage having come straight from the house and seats herself, perplexed by her own encounter with Olivia. Immediately

Malvolio appears from the same U entrance; still 'running', he is tiring visibly (laugh 2); he 'runs' down to the R corner of the stage and stops; he looks out towards the audience 'Where can he be? – not there.' He 'runs' across below Cesario to the L (laugh 2), and is about to exit when he becomes aware that Cesario has risen and is now standing. It looks like him, but is it? I point the top end of my staff: 'Were not *you* e'en now with the Countess Olivia?' 'On a *moderate* pace I have since arrived but hither.' (Is that a veiled criticism that he walks faster than I run?) However, 'She returns this ring to you, sir.' The staff regains its normal vertical position but upside down – damned thing! Reverse it, embarrassing (laugh 1), and again couched at the left elbow to facilitate the removal of the ring while saying, 'You might have saved me my pains to have taken it away yourself.' But the ring has stuck (laugh 3). A heave. No good. A quick look to Cesario, don't let him think I am embarrassed; 'She adds moreover that you should put your Lord into a desperate' (that word is coloured by his own desperation) 'assurance she will none of him.' Another tug and an attempt to unscrew the ring – but it is still stuck. What a terrible thing to happen! (Laugh 5.) But play for time: 'And one thing more . . . ' The mind has raced: he remembers his mother removing a ring by sucking it and the surrounding finger and so lubricating it; he does so. He succeeds, and by the end of 'unless it be to report your Lord's taking of this' it is off! – 'Receive it so.' I hold it out at arm's length with R hand finger tips, but Cesario says, 'She took the ring of me, I'll none of it' and he crosses D R. Out of all patience I shout, 'Come, sir!' He turns back. 'You *peevishly* threw it to her and her will is it should be *so*' (i.e. 'peevishly') 'returned' (laugh 4). Affecting a 'peevish' stance, L foot raised and L arm half-raised for a rather feminine throw he inadvertently appears effeminate as he throws the ring at Cesario's feet. Cesario makes no move. 'If it be worth the stooping for, there it lies [lays] in your eye [aye]; if not, be it his' (and I know very well that *you* will pick it up the moment I am out of sight) 'that "finds" it.' Staff to the horizontal position and I eject myself into the air to continue 'running' – Upstage. It takes three or four steps to realize that I no longer have to run; put on the brakes! A quick look back to glare at Cesario for a moment of embarrassment (laugh 4) which of course *I* won't admit and with more dignity than at any other time in the play I stride, like a galleon in full sail, straight U and off centre.

Lying in bed that night, having read a few pages of St Thomas Aquinas and wondering what attitude to take to the proposed new Prayer Book, at around midnight I hear sounds coming from the garden; they increase in volume: what is it – a riot? I leap out of bed wearing my new nightgown. It reaches just to my knees. Slippers on, putting my chain of office around my neck, symbol of authority, what would I be without it? my fur-collared coat over the top and my hat on my head – it's a cold night and I *am* bald – I race off down the stairs and out to the garden. I can now see Sir Toby and Maria dancing and singing while Feste plays his wretched guitar and Sir Andrew his bagpipes!! At my very fastest walk I eject myself from the R (in fact I always stood several paces offstage at the 'start' position in order to achieve maximum propulsion at the moment of entry onstage). Arriving in the centre of the group, Feste on my left, Aguecheek D C, Sir Toby U C and Maria standing on the chair R, the 'music' continues until one by one they become aware of my presence (laugh 8); first Feste, then Maria who signals to Toby who sits C, then Aguecheek who subsides on to the floor. Again, John Barton disapproved of the hat in this scene, but I felt it quite legitimate to wear it. Malvolio would have felt undressed without hat *and* coat. I am furious! Passing my glower from Aguecheek back to Feste I suddenly become aware that my coat has flown open exposing my 'shorty' nightgown and my bare legs beneath it! With a lightning movement I cross the coat over my shame (at the same moment one knee slightly crosses the other resulting in an 'unintentional' attitude of effeminacy (laugh 6) – a middle-aged Susannah surprised at her bath). A snatched look at them all – did they see my nightgown? I cannot openly attack Sir Toby or Sir Andrew, but I can attack Feste and Maria, my minions, and through them the other two, so I address Feste. He has gone too far. Far too far. I walk above him to C and strike an attitude, left hand on the back of the deck-chair and right hand pulls back my coat and rests on my right hip (laugh 6). Quite forgetting that I now expose nightgown and legs and look totally absurd while telling Sir Toby I must be round with him. Sir Toby and Feste are untamed. Right, then – I will break it up by removing their supplies. Andrew has placed his drinking vessel on the floor as he subsided, so on my way to collect it, moving round L and D C, I pass Feste and say, 'Is it even so?' (if it is, that is your lot). I pick it up – Good God! it is one of my Lady's best glass goblets. I say to Sir Andrew, 'This is much credit to you.' I take the glass U and behind the table where I find that they have *all* been using glass goblets – not only that, but also one of my Lady's best decanters and a silver tray and a silver candelabra on which are burning *three* candles. They cost a great deal of money and I am responsible for the household accounts! This will never happen again! I pick up the tray and all its contents. Suddenly I hear Sir Toby at my L saying, 'Art any more than a steward?' My lips tighten, my eyes narrow (stop before you go too far). 'Rub your chain with crumbs', he says, and 'A stoop of wine, Maria.' My chance. He cannot, he shall not, involve *my* servants. My head lashes round to Maria who is about to follow Sir Toby's request. 'Mistress Mary' is spoken quietly but menacingly; there is no doubt about it meaning 'stand still'. 'She shall know of it' (tell-tale) 'by this hand.' A final sneer at them all – particularly Sir Toby, for my last remarks were as much for his benefit as Maria's; my head erect, tray held carefully, sharp R turn I march off R (an imperceptible half step backwards before L, R, L, R) (laugh 5).

I like to think that the letter scene (2.5) was originally played with Toby, Andrew and Fabian (where does he spring from?) hidden in the upper balcony over an inner stage. Maria could then get a laugh with, 'Get you all three into the box – tree.' The box tree has been treated in different ways; sometimes three individual trees can be carried round the stage, and sometimes there is a series of trees with the three moving from one to another. In this production Maria placed the letter on a deck-chair and the spectators hid behind a hedge (breaking the convention which normally does not allow soliloquy to be overheard by other characters). Barton thought of it as Malvolio's scene and left him the rest of the stage unencumbered. When we began work on the scene we found we had to give some thought to the letter. What type of letter? A scroll? A single sheet? Folded? – once, twice? All we know is that it is 'sealed' – or has upon it a seal. I spent some time devising 'my' letter; and after several attempts evolved the version shown in Fig. 7. I will explain why as we go.

Malvolio has been strolling in the garden and even loosened the neck of his tunic! ('Practising behaviour to his own shadow' I took to mean 'As his only audience' rather than 'Making shadow-shapes'.) His arms behind his back at waist level he appears U C but looking off L as Maria says 'for here comes the trout that must be caught with tickling', before leaving. He walks very slowly straight D C imperiously surveying his domain. Half-way down he involuntarily breaks into a little dance step (feet only) (laugh 3). I had in fact learnt the step for *Henry VIII* from which it had eventually been cut and I thought it a pity to waste it! Suddenly the thought that he may be seen stops him and almost in panic looks, quickly, first L, and then R, into the exits. No, all is well; so proceed D C. Arriving below the hedge his attention is caught by something L; it is 'my Lady' in imagination. He effects a most elaborate bow and extends his L hand on which to place 'hers', gives 'her' a sickly, ingratiating smile and 'they' turn to move R but – who is that skulking in the shadows D R? (One of the common people.)

Jove knows I love : but who?
Lips do not moue : No man must know.
I may command where I adore,
But silence like a Lucrece knife
With bloodless stroke my heart doth gore;
M.O.A.I. doth sway my life.

If this fall into thy hand, revolue. In my stars I am
aboue thee, but bee not afraid of greatnes: some are born
great, some achieue greatnes, and some haue greatnes
thrust vpon them.

Thy fates open their hands, cast thy humble slough and
appear fresh.

Be opposite with a kinsman, surly with seruants, let thy tongue
tang arguments of state : put thyself into the trick of
singularity. She thus aduises thee that sighs for thee.

Remember who commended thy yellow stockings, and wished to
see thee euer crossgartered : I say remember. Go to, thou art
made if thou desirest to be so : if not, let me see thee a
steward still, the fellow of seruants, and not worthy to
touch Fortune's fingers.

Farewell. She that would alter seruices with thee.

                    The Fortunate Unhappy

Thou canst not choose but know who I am : If thou entertain'st my love, let it appear in thy smiling, thy smiles become thee well. Therefore in my presence still smile, dear, O my sweet, I prithee.

To the Unknown Beloved

This and my Good Wishes

X

SM

7 Malvolio's letter

He glowers, his R hand shoots out and an imperious finger beckons the varlet – 'he' approaches – the finger gestures 'him' to kneel – 'he' doesn't – the glower deepens – again 'Down' says the finger. 'He' kneels. Malvolio draws an imaginary sword and violently decapitates him, replaces sword and smiles benignly on his 'consort' (laugh 3). Such is power! This has evoked a laugh and to his great consternation he is aware that he *is* overlooked by the theatre audience. Horror; his left arm is still holding 'my Lady's' imaginary hand! Consternation: this requires an explanation. ' 'Tis but fortune – *all* is fortune.' (The following part of the line I found terribly ambiguous; 'Maria once told me she did affect me and I have heard herself' etc. sounds as if 'she' and 'herself' applied to Maria rather than to Olivia. John Barton suggested I should say, 'Maria once told me my Lady did affect me', which certainly clarifies it though the purists will object.) 'It should be one of *my complexion*' (of which he is very proud!), and on that happy note he can amble R above the chair on which he places his L hand. 'What should I think on't?' causes him to move slightly D R. A smile breaks; his eyes narrow and glisten, 'To be *Count* Malvolio'. The audience have laughed at Andrew and Toby's following lines as he is about to sit on the chair on which the letter has been placed. Malvolio thinks the audience must be laughing at him; he is arrested in a half-sit – 'There is *example* for't. The Lady of the Strachy married the Yeoman of the Wardrobe' – so there. He completes the action of sitting and becomes involved in his reverie – 'Having been three months married to her, sitting', as thus, 'in my state' – while Toby speaks, Malvolio notices his 'officers' off R and gestures them forward, 'calling my officers about me, in my branched velvet gown', described with a gesture 'having come from a day bed where I have left *Olivia*', and such is my prowess – he looks at a knowing colleague in the circle – '*sleeping*', his eyebrows flicker to underline his point (laugh 4). 'And then' with Olivia safely tucked up, 'to have the *humour* of state; and after a demure travel of regard', he looks along the circle from L to R and selects one person to whom to address with an accusatory finger, 'telling them I know my place as I would they should do theirs, to ask for my *kinsman*' (as he is now!) 'Toby' (that pig). A slight pause and he rolls the letter into a 'tube'; 'I frown the while and perchance . . . wind up my watch . . . or play with my . . .' The letter is now held upright on his lap somewhat suggestively; the audience is about to giggle (laugh 3) – (filthy minds these people have) – an explanation is necessary, 'some rich jewel' (laugh 2). 'Toby approaches' from L, '*curtsies* there to me . . . I extend my hand to him thus', an imperious L hand is extended palm down and as an afterthought he adds, 'quenching my familiar *smile* with an austere regard of control' (laugh 2) (why should they think that funny?). 'You *MUST* amend your drunkenness', the head relaxes slightly R but cracks back with, '*Besides*; you waste the treasure of your time with a foolish knight . . . one Sir *Andrew*' (a second-class Christian name). The daydream is over; his attention wanders; what is this in his hand? A piece of paper; put it where? Down beside the chair – someone else will clear it up. But – it has writing upon it – 'What employment have we here?' The writing is upside down, he turns it round.

'*BY MY LIFE*': he leaps from the chair and speaks directly to the audience 'this is may Lady's hand!' He studies the writing and finds confirmation. He shows the writing to the audience and illustrates with his L hand 'These be her very c's, her u's 'n her t's' (Naughtily I abbreviated the original text of 'and her t's'), 'and *thus* makes she her great P's' (laugh 3). I must forestall the audience's reaction. Malvolio doesn't intend the bawdry, but Shakespeare does (there is no 'c' or 'P' in the superscription). He throws the letter aside and starts to move U. His eyes roam the audience (I would not dream of reading someone else's letter). His fingers run along the back of the chair R to L. As it reaches the end . . . did his foot slip? or how is it that he has now lost 18 inches in height and has the back of the chair under his R armpit? (laugh 4). He can now read the superscription, 'To the unknown beloved, this, and my good wishes'. As he picks it up and moves D C he tells the onlookers, 'Her very phrases . . . By your leave'. (Excuse me for a

8   The folded letter

To the Unknown Beloued

This and my Good Wishes

X

55

moment while I open this.) But there is a great seal. Foiled! Showing it to the audience who will now understand the reason for this stoppage he says, 'Wax' (laugh 2) and illustrates with a finger. 'Soft' (therefore only recently sealed!), 'and the impressure *her* Lucrece.' As he squeezes the sides of the letter so that it resembles a telescope, he says, 'With which she uses to seal. '*Tis* may Lady.' After asking, 'To whom should this be?' with one eye closed he peers through it as if it were the most natural way of reading a letter (laugh 1); again he fails to discover the contents. The letter is now flat again. He tries to raise one corner of the flap, now the other corner, and the

9 The partly unfolded letter

Jove knows J loue: but who?
Lips do not moue: No man must know.
J may command where J adore,
But silence like a Lucrece knife
With bloodless stroke my heart doth gore;
M.O.A.J. doth sway my life.

Thou canst not choose but know who J am:
If thou entertainest my loue, let it appear in thy
smiling, thy smiles become thee well. Therefore in my
presence still smile, O my sweet, J prithee.

wax gives way! He emits a high-pitched, almost effeminate 'Oh' (laugh 4) (or what is shorter than 'Oh'? 'O'?). As he looks at the audience (what an awful thing to happen) the look develops into a 'You will probably think that I did that on purpose.' A *third* of the letter is snatched open . . .

The postscript is upside down so is impossible to read. What meets his eye is 'Jove knows I love, but who? Lips, do not move. No man must knoo' (laugh 2). Incredulous he repeats, 'No man must *knoo?*'; to the audience (silly me) 'No man must know!' Ah. 'If this should be thee . . . Malvolio'. You will notice that I cut 'What follows? The numbers altered.' Arrogantly I thought this gives away the MOAI point too soon, and I inserted 'What follows?' before reciting in a tee-tum, tee-tum fashion:

> I may command where I adore
> But silence like a Lucrece knife
> With bloodless stroke my heart doth gore
> Moai doth sway my life.

And puzzled, I ask if the audience know the word – 'MO–AH–EE?' (laugh 2). While Fabian and Sir Toby speak I try to work it out; ' "MO–AH–EE doth sway my life." Nay, but first let me see, let me see'; the next two lines being cut he continues, ' "I may command where I adore." Why, she may command me', he tells the audience, 'I serve her; she is may Lady. Why this is evident to any formal capacity, there is *no* obstruction in this' – spoken so quickly it elicits a laugh. 'What should that alphabetical position portend? If I could make that resemble something in *me* . . . "M" comma "O" comma "A" comma', and he shows the commas to the audience the while; what a fool he has been not to notice before! So what does it all mean? 'M', he queries. A great light dawns. The eyes pop. The 'M' dissolves into 'M' m M A L V O L I O', he ventures in a whisper. Don't they understand?' ' "M" . . . why, that begins MY NAME!' So that is clear for the 'M', 'but then there is no *consonancy*' (no consonants) 'in the sequel. That *suffers* under probation . . . "A" *should* follow but "O" *does*! The "I" comes behind.' More thought: ' "M.O.A.I" ' etc.

After picking out the word 'crush', the other third of the letter falls open. 'Soft!' A silencing finger is raised while his R hand holds the letter, 'here follows *prose*'. (Thank God, after all that poesy.) 'If this fall into thy hand, revolve'; a look at the audience, 'it can't mean that! If it does, I *won't*.' But as he continues he involuntarily walks in a tight circle, making sure that the resulting laugh (3) does not obscure the lines. 'In my stars I am above thee, but be not afraid of greatness; some are *born* great' (not me) 'some achieve greatness' (not me) 'and some' (wait for it) 'have greatness *thrust upon 'em*.'

He flashes a plea to the audience. Do they understand the importance of that? His speech now becomes faster and faster, growing in excitement as the truths reveal themselves. 'Remember who commended thy yellow stockings' (yellow stockings, to the audience) 'and wished to see thee ever cross-gartered' (cross-*gartered*?). 'I say remember. Go to, thou art *made* if thou desir'st to be so. If *not*, let me see thee a . . .' (does it? Yes it does! Joy can know no bounds!) – to the gallery, 'STEWARD still.' They obviously don't believe him, so he shows them the *very* word and mouths it a second time (laugh 3). Fools! He is patently wasting his time on them – they only laugh. 'The fellow of servants and not worthy to touch fortune's finger farewell she that would alter services with thee the fortunate unhappy.' He is breathless (so am I), but up, up, *exultant*, 'Daylight and champagne discover not more. *This is open.*' He strikes the letter on 'this' and on 'open'. Right, then! 'I *will* be *proud*. I will *read politic authors*. I will *baffle Sir Toby*. I will wash off *gross acquaintance*. I will be *point devise* the *very man*!' The voice drops in pitch and intensity and slowly begins to rise again, 'I do not now fool myself to let *imagination* jade me; for every *reason* excites to *this* . . . that *may Lady, loves*, ME!' The voice drops again, only to rise again, 'I thank my stars' (and there they are somewhere above the gallery); 'I . . . am . . . *Happy*' (laugh 3) and never has a face looked more gloomy although ecstatic. So, resolved and fast, 'I will be *strange, stout, in yellow stockings* and cross-gartered' (if that is the way She wants it) 'even with the swiftness of putting on.' He turns to run upstage but before taking a step he turns back and down on one knee, 'Jove and my stars be praised', he crosses himself (laugh 2). Oh! A quick look at the populace, 'don't think that I just crossed myself', and he is off upstage looking down at the letter. A scream! 'Ahhhhhhh', he turns and beckons to the audience: 'Here', and by way of explanation he races back to a 'friend' who happens to be sitting in the front row of the stalls and shows him, 'is yet a postscript!' (laugh 2). (All right. I'll read it to you.) 'Thou can'st not choose but *know who I am*! If thou entertainst my love, let it appear in thy *smiling* . . .' a squeal of brakes – poleaxed! (laugh 2). Look for a friend – None? (Gloomily.) 'Thy *smiles* become thee well, therefore in my presence still *smile*.' The word becomes 'manure', the mouth a gash; 'dear, O my sweet, I prithee'. Total dejection! – but mounting larks should sing. There is iron resolution in this man, so in the voice of Job he calls upon his God, '*Jove! I thank thee! I will* "smile"' (and what is more I'll try it now) – the corners of the mouth extend some two inches towards his ears, but that is all (laugh 3). He can do it. Given time. 'I will do everything that Thou' – and his extended arm nearly touches Jove himself – 'wilt have me!' Malvolio floats swiftly upstage and off (laugh 9 and round of applause).

I don't mind admitting that I used to collapse sweating in my dressing-room. The necessary ebullience was the most ecstatic I have yet been able to produce as an actor. In my Malvolio wardrobe I find a pair of black and yellow slashed breeches; they are Elizabethan rather than Jacobean, however. And here is a large yellow ruff, and a hat – very similar to my other but with a wide brim. With today's top-lighting in the theatre this would shadow the face, so the designer agreed that the front of the brim should be flattened and attached to the crown. This is topped by a large yellow feather. Our designer pointed out that cross-gartering merely implied that the normal garter, from below the knee, was crossed at the back of the leg and continued up and round again above the knee before being tied in a bow. Never having attempted this before, Malvolio has tied

10   'If this fall into thy hand, revolve'

them far too tight and they are serving as a tourniquet, a fact that is to colour the whole scene. He has spent some hours creeping around the house and garden in an endeavour to find Olivia. Is she evading him? And he must try not to be seen by the servants. The gaiety with which he donned the garments is now wearing rather thin – was it, will it be, worth this masquerade? Where can she be? My legs are killing me. Legs which were so straight, almost knock-kneed, are now bowed with the agony. I have literally to hold on to the gatepost U C as I am about to come down into the garden (laugh 6).

Shakespeare very cleverly allowed his Malvolio to be totally outrageous in this scene, excusing all by making Fabian say 'If this were played upon a stage now, I could condemn it for an improbable fiction.'

My face is grimacing with the pain. I hobble forward and half-way down (laugh 4) and there she is! – standing D R with her back to me. Pull myself together, the pain has gone! or has it? Twinges every now and again, I make my way to the L of the sundial – I can lean on it if necessary. I 'prepare' myself for the total effect. I have her letter in my L hand – both arms are lifted effectively above my head; I succeed in looking rather like the famous Faun of Pompeii and filled with the same euphoria. But she doesn't turn! (Maria is there L but I don't see her.) A discreet cough. She turns! 'How now, Malvolio?'; not *quite* the reaction I expected; but of course! I have forgotten the smile! Here goes (laugh 4). Very musically, almost sung, 'Sweet Lady', and then – as written – flatly, with no humour at all, 'Ho. Ho' (laugh 4). The parallel fingers of my R hand punctuate both 'Ho's' like castanets; Burbage never produced such an effect! 'I sent for thee upon a sad occasion', she will have her little jokes; 'Sad, Lady? I could *be* sad . . . This', I lift my L leg and point to it, 'does make some obstruction in the blood' (the increased pressure on the R leg causes me to clutch, and lean on the sundial) (laugh 5), 'but what of that? – If it please the eye of one, it is with me as the very true sonnet is, "Please one and please all".' (John Barton discovered that this was a lyric of a popular song of the time so I attempted to sing it, unmusically, while illustrating that 'one' applied to Olivia and 'all' to the audience.) 'Not *black* in my *mind* though *yellow* in my *legs*' (laugh 2); my best joke for years! I fail to notice that *no one* laughs at it. I hold the letter aloft; 'It did come to his hands and commands shall be executed! I think we do know the sweet Roman hand'; and I speak as one who can recognize a Gill Sans Serif at ten paces as I face away to peruse the contents of the letter. (In reality, to allow myself the required reaction on the next line.) WHAT has she said?! My reaction is shock. Horror. Panic (laugh 7). The audience see him in full face. 'To bed?' Good God! So soon? But what must be must be: 'AY!' (laugh 4) is a battle cry: the challenge is accepted, '*Sweet heart* and I'll come to thee.' Valentino was never in better form: endless kisses are exploded and my finger tips flick them in her direction. Suddenly from my left, the voice of Maria. How dare she! I am committed. I must play this through. 'Be surly with servants' – 'At *your* request?! Yessss', what do I mean by that? – I don't know, but it gives me time to think my next quip: 'Nightingales answer daws', and a glance at Olivia for approbation. But Maria goes on. She must be quelled. I will quote to her a line which should be to her totally incomprehensible while at the same time impressing 'may Lady', so, in portentous tones (Abandon Hope All Ye, etc.), 'Be not afraid of greatness', and a quick aside to Olivia, ''twas well writ' (laugh 1). Oh goody. Olivia is joining in the game, pretending she doesn't understand, so with rising tones 'some are *born* great, some *achieve* greatness, and some have greatness *thrust upon* them' (laugh 2). I don't hear her intervening lines; I now take her by the arm and cross L. I will show her that I have memorized every word of her letter and at the same time sweep her off her feet to a climactic 'If *not*, let me see thee a *servant* still!' (laugh 3). Unbeknown, a servant has entered behind me L and as I open my mouth to say – perhaps – 'Madam *this is it*', he says 'Madam, the young gentleman of the Count Orsino's is returned.' I register him but I am now sitting on a cloud – nothing can deflate me. They all exit.

'Oh ho' is triumphant and straight at the audience, 'do you come near me now!' 'Cast thy humble slough' is from memory, but while I speak I open the letter and read – for proof positive – the rest of the quotation. I cut the next twenty-eight words because in the letter as we have it 'sad face', 'slow tongue', 'reverend carriage' are not mentioned at all. Also, theatrically I was able to leapfrog to 'I have limed her! but' (of course I must not forget) 'it is *Jove's* doing and, Jove!' (a call to attract His attention just above the back row of the gallery) 'make me thankful.' I address the audience again – orchestra stalls now, 'and when she went away now, "Let this *fellow* be looked to"' (you realize the importance of that?). I look around – surely *someone* out there does! Idiots! '"*Fel low*"' (laugh 2); they still don't get it, 'not *Malvolio*, nor after my degree, but FELLOW' (laugh 3).

I am saddened to record that it took me nearly a hundred performances to evolve the next piece of 'business'. The turning-point was a matinée in Adelaide while we were on a tour of Australia. The local company, whose performance of *The Seagull* we had seen the week before, came to the *Twelfth Night* matinée. I tried to think of something that, while not in any way disturbing the rest of the audience, might please a very charming group of fellow Thespians. I was quite unprepared for the result – one of the best laughs in the play. As I have stated, bang in the centre of the stage was a designer's gimmick: a sundial – all very charming but of no use at all; all movements were restricted to circling round it. I had already discovered some use for it in the succeeding part of the scene, of which more anon, but I now thought that if the disc at the end of my chain were a watch and if at this moment I were to look at the time indicated on the sundial and if on checking my watch against it I should find a variance, Malvolio's meticulous mind would automatically assume that his watch would be correct and that it was the sundial that showed the incorrect time. It should be therefore put to rights. The sundial, being made of stone, would be heavy, but under pressure could be twisted (I tried it on a real one and unless cemented to the ground it can be done). So, I assume the sun to be shining from the R corner at the back of the gallery. 'Why everything adheres together' (glance at sundial) 'that no dram of a scruple' (look at watch) 'no scruple of a scruple' (back to sundial) 'no obstacle' (look at watch). Check 'sunbeam' to sundial and adjust it until correct time is shown during – 'no incredulous or unsafe circumstance' (laugh 9).

But who comes here? Toby. Begin as I mean to go on: complete *hauteur*. I hear him but am heedless of his words. As Toby says 'How is't with you?' he attempts to lay a soothing hand on my right forearm – how dare he! I knock it away as one would a mosquito one hears approaching the face and bring my hand sharply back to nearly where it was, but impale it upon the finger of the sundial! – 'Ah!' (laugh 5). It is pure trickery: the flat of the hand merely strikes the angle of the 'finger'. In considerable pain Malvolio shakes his hand, looks at the wound and determines to brave it out, but Sir Toby, startled, produces a crude crucifix and advises Malvolio to 'defy the devil'. In his confused, euphoric state Malvolio believes this drunkard to be embarking on a theological dissertation – 'Do you know what you say?' is a rhetorical reprimand. It is all too much: the euphoria, the agony of the cross-gartering, the pain of the impaled hand, the insults; one must make a good exit, hence 'Geow. Hang yourselves all! You are idle shellow things. I am not of your element. You shall know more hereafter' is split between my adversaries (laugh 3). Malvolio turns, but the tourniquet has done its work, his R leg has quite gone to sleep, he nearly falls, staggers and hobbles in great pain U C and off.

I will admit to a dissatisfaction on this exit – I never really succeeded in bringing it off theatrically, even if I did truthfully.

Apart from the almost incidental 'We'll have him in a dark room and bound' Shakespeare in no way prepares his audience for the shock of Malvolio's next appearance. The play was written when bull- and bear-baiting were common sports, the pillory entertained jeering crowds, idiots were part of 'the public stock of harmless pleasure' and the populace thronged to public executions. In John Barton's production, the so-called prison scene took place somewhere at the end of the garden where there could have been some type of primitive septic tank covered firstly by an iron grille and over that a trap door to keep out some of the disgusting smell. In this Malvolio has been placed. We are to imagine that the floor of this sewer is some eight feet below ground level, so only by gripping the bars and pulling himself up will Malvolio be able to just get his head through the bars. His hands and head will be the only parts visible.

Feste stamps on the trap. Who, what is it? 'Oh!' Feste opens the trap as he says 'What ho I say, peace in this prison.' Are 'they' about to taunt him again? Defensively, 'Who calls there?' It is practically dark outside but the faintest glimmer of moonlight attracts Malvolio as he grips the bar and pulls his head through (laugh 4); his eyes are starting from his head, he is hysterical. 'Good Sir Topas. Do not think I am mad' (but I think I am) – 'they have laid me here in *hideous darkness*', and Malvolio is weeping. 'Say'st thou that house is dark?' 'As *Hell*, Sir Topas.' Hell to Malvolio is a very real place, but Sir Topas then tells Malvolio that the clerestories are 'lustrous as ebony'. Malvolio looks from R slowly to L, trying to fathom what to a sane man is nonsense but to him is surely proof of his own madness. Like King Lear's 'Let me not be mad!' Malvolio then slowly and tearfully tells himself, 'I . . . am . . . not . . . mad . . . Sir . . . Topas', and clinging to reason, 'I say to you this house is *dark*!' In reply to Sir Topas, Malvolio then explodes, 'I say this house is as dark as ignorance though ignorance were as dark as hell and I say there was never man thus *abused*.' That spurt has exhausted Malvolio who realizes that he is merely antagonizing Sir Topas; the tears are held back, 'I am no more mad than you are – make the trial of it in any constant question.' (I am not mad. I am not mad. I am not mad.) 'What is the opinion of Pythagoras concerning wildfowl?' Ah, I know, I know the answer! 'That the soul of our grandam might haply inhabit a bird.' 'What thinkest thou of his opinion?' As a true Catholic, 'I think nobly of the soul and no way approve his opinion.' During his next line Feste makes to lower the trap door; Malvolio is aware of this manoeuvre; he is to be left to the rats and spiders. Sheer panic sets in. His last chance is going. While crying 'No. No. No', Malvolio tries to ward off the closing trap. 'Sir Topas, Sir Topas', are hardly 'words', but pleas running into sobs.

For what must seem hours Malvolio is left until a voice is heard – is that Feste? 'Fool?' It *is*! 'Fool!' He hasn't heard me! 'Fool!! I say!!' Feste lifts the trap and at the same instant Malvolio hauls himself up like a drowning man clutching the bars, causing Feste to back hastily R and fall to his knees; 'Who calls, ha?' As if there had never been any misunderstanding between them, Malvolio continues, 'Good Fool, as ever thou wilt deserve well at my hand, help me to a *candle*!' Malvolio's voice breaks – this is the nearest he comes to admitting his terror of the dark, 'and pen, ink and paper'; no answer. 'As I am a gentleman' (and as soon as I get out of here) 'I will live to be thankful to thee for't.' Feste advances on his knees cautiously. 'Master Malvolio?' I can quite understand that he would never recognize me in this condition, but, believe it or not, it *is* me: 'Aye, good Fool.' Thank God, he seems to understand. 'Fool, there was never man so notoriously abused'; and as one sane man to another, 'I am as well in my wits, Fool, as thou art.' I am unable to take in his reply. My predicament dominates all. 'They have here propertied me. Keep me in darkness.' (Each time on that word the voice breaks and the body shudders.) 'Send ministers to me!' 'Asses!' is screamed off to the L. The exertion is again too much. 'And do all they can to face me out of my wits', is deflated.

Feste has apparently seen someone and with 'Advise you what you say' he seems to indicate that I should hide. I drop to the bottom of the pit out of sight. It sounds like the priest! 'Sir Topas' – my words are cautious yet accusatory; apparent silence; the priest has gone, I can now come up; but has Feste gone? Please God no. 'Fool! . . . Fool!! . . . Fool, I say !!!', panic again. But he is still there. 'Good fool; help me to some *light*!'; Malvolio is weak and near to collapse, 'and some paper.' 'I tell thee' (and myself) 'I am as well in my wits as any man in Illyria', but he doesn't believe me. As a lion's paw that would drag a victim through the bars of its cage a hand whips out and grabs Feste, all of whose strength is needed to prevent his being pulled through the grille. 'By this hand I *am*!' Where did that vicious strength come from? Feste whimpers. But again the exertion is too much and the relapse greater. Now I have alienated him, too – he never liked me in the first place – he is sure to take revenge. '*Good* Fool' is now a begging for forgiveness, 'some ink, paper and' (pl*ease*) '*light*; and convey what I will set down to may Lady.' I don't think I have succeeded in winning him over – perhaps bribery? 'It shall advantage thee more than ever the bearing of letter did.' He is abject. Feste agrees but asks two questions which are answered consecutively, '*Believe* me', with the voice breaking, it is almost the prayer of a sinner, 'I am not'; their heads move from side to side to underline the statement. 'I tell thee true', my grip is relaxed; Feste makes one more taunt but extricates himself at the same time and eludes the claws which futilely try to catch him again. How I dislike that man. Hypocritically I call after him 'Fool, I'll requite it in the highest degree.' A nod of dismissal – for God's sake, go! – but I mustn't upset him – 'I *prithee*, be gone.' Feste picks up his guitar and begins inexplicably to sing! What is he saying? He has tricked me! As the song gets faster and faster he begins to run round and round the trap, back and forth, across the grille, over my head; I try to follow the direction of his antics; the world swims; I *am* mad; faster and faster; round and round; a mumbled series of cries which could be defined as 'No. No. . No. . . No. . . No. . . No. . .'; I am still holding myself up by the bars; Feste stamps on my hands; I hold on; he slams the trap closed while my head is apparently still in view above the grille; with a scream I fall to the bottom of the pit. Silence; daylight comes; Sebastian enters, 'Yet 'tis not madness.' A very weak cry of 'Help' comes from below ground, unheard by Sebastian, 'That this may be some error but no madness'. An almost incoherent sentence containing the word 'help' is heard. Sebastian talks on, 'To any other trust but that I am mad'. A faint sound of nonsensical gibberish can be heard trailing off into sobs.

I will admit that I would not have liked this interpolation had I been playing Sebastian, but John Barton allowed me to produce this most terrifying effect.

In the next scene Malvolio speaks verse, and continues to do so through the rest of the play. Why? Is it that in this most poetic of plays he is a very prosaic character? Certainly the use of verse in this last scene is extremely valuable to the actor because it is easier to 'take off'.

Malvolio is as mad as it is possible for a sane man to be. Hours later Fabian and another have been sent to release Malvolio and escort him to the presence of Olivia. They try to control him – how dare they touch me! With a bellow like a wounded bull Malvolio erupts through the centre entrance (laugh 5). A large number of people are gathered. Oblivious, Malvolio has eyes only to seek out Olivia. There she is D R. He staggers forward and there is no one else present for him, as he explodes (from C) 'Madam, you have done me wrong, / *Notorious* wrong!' She contradicts: I have now nothing to lose, so can answer back 'Lady, you *have*. Pray you peruse that letter'; she takes it, 'You must not now deny it is your hand' (look at it!), 'Or say 'tis not your seal' (look at it!), 'not your invention. / You can say *none* of this. Well' (have the grace to) 'grant it then, / And tell me – in the modesty of honour, / Why you have given me such clear lights of favour . . .' But soon he falters and begins to break down, '*Why* have you suffered me to be *imprisoned*, / Kept in a *dark* house' – this line he tells to the others who are standing L (she did that to me); 'visited by the priest', a maniacal look around – (where is he!), 'And made the most notorious geck and gull / That e'er invention played on.' He can hardly get the words out through the sobs – '*Tell me* – why?'

'This is not my writing', she says. Malvolio snatches the letter and looks at it – of course it's her writing; 'But out of question 'tis Maria's hand.' Malvolio's jaw drops, the eyes start; an 'Ugh!' (meaning What!) and he checks every word of the letter. Can this be so? It is so – Fabian confirms it is. As he unravels the story Malvolio sinks to his knees and sobs. As Fabian finishes, an attempt at a plea of justification breaks out as, 'I – I – I', which Olivia assuages with, 'Alas, poor fool'. And now Feste rams the knife home, he kneels R beside the kneeling Malvolio and sadistically twists the knife. He was in the plot. He was Sir Topas. My own words are thrown in my face, but there is no fight left in Malvolio, he can only await the *coup de grâce*: 'And thus the whirligig of time brings in his revenges.' Malvolio staggers to his feet and the wounded bull looks about him. They are smiling at him, a kindly smile. But the degradation is too great; so, pathetically like a small boy who knows he has lost but cannot leave without an exit line, says to them all '*I'll* be revenged', he pauses and pouts, 'on the whole *pack* of you.' It is a totally empty threat. The House, Illyria, the World, will shortly be laughing at his predicament. I believe there is but one thing for Malvolio – suicide.

Orlando in
As You Like It

JOHN BOWE

BEFORE joining the Royal Shakespeare Company in 1978, John Bowe had played a variety of parts, including Dunois in the Prospect production of *Saint Joan* and Iago in the New Shakespeare Company's *Othello*. At Stratford, his parts have ranged from Corporal Taylor in *The Churchill Play*, Jack Skipper in *Captain Swing*, and Black Will in *Arden of Faversham* (all, initially, at The Other Place) to his Shakespearean roles at the Royal Shakespeare Theatre. Between 1978 and 1983 he has appeared there as Gratiano, Orlando, Laertes, Mowbray, Ratcliffe, the King of France (in *King Lear*) and Tranio, repeating many of these roles in seasons at Newcastle, the Aldwych, the Warehouse and the Barbican. He has also arranged fights for some Royal Shakespeare Company productions. He first played Orlando in the 1980 season, with Susan Fleetwood as Rosalind and Sinead Cusack as Celia. The production, designed by Farrah, was directed by Terry Hands.

From the outset *As You Like It* was to be a fairy tale. A boy, Orlando, meets a girl, Rosalind, and each falls instantaneously in love with the other. The boy undergoes a trial of his manhood against the champion of the wicked Duke, and wins. Both are the children of enemies of the Duke and out of fear for their lives each runs away to the comparative safety of the forest, where eventually they discover each other again, marry and supposedly live happily ever after. This was Terry Hands's guideline for our production.

My initial problems in attempting to make my Orlando a part of this fairy tale were weight, age and innocence. I lost a stone in weight, gave up smoking (at last!), shaved off my beard and worked hard at raising the range of my voice. So much for the exterior, but what about the way this earthy young man saw the world? Terry helped me to discover this when he took us to see an old silent movie called *Tramp, Tramp, Tramp* starring

11 'Wit, whither wilt?'
John Bowe as Orlando and Susan Fleetwood as Rosalind, March 1980

Harry Langdon. I think he wanted us to see just how far you can go and yet still retain the sympathies of an audience. Here was the perfect example, Harry Langdon, with white face and baby-like mannerisms, making us laugh, and quite beautifully moving us to tears. He was outrageous and yet truthful, coy and cheeky, but charmingly so. Just as, in a cartoon, animators can make us willingly suspend our disbelief in a talking mouse, so an actor can make an audience willingly suspend their disbelief in a make-believe world of wicked dukes and boys dressed up as girls, or was it the other way round?

So I had this energetic but shy young man, suppressed by his eldest brother, Oliver, since his father's death. No bad thing, perhaps, since it meant his life was spent nearer to Nature. Throughout rehearsal and performance I felt more and more that this was of importance to the balance of Rosalind and Orlando's relationship. She, from the court, well-mannered, well-educated, with hands no doubt perfumed with civet; he, rustically kept, ill-educated, and condemned to a life of servitude. Indeed, the comparisons of a life at court to a life in the country run through the play; in the first forest-lord scene:

Now my co-mates and brothers in exile,
Hath not old custom made this life more sweet
Than that of painted pomp? Are not these woods
More free from peril than the envious court? (2.1.1–4)

And in Touchstone's debate with Corin:

TOUCHSTONE Why, if thou never wast at court, thou never saw'st good manners;
if thou never saw'st good manners, then thy manners must be wicked,
and wickedness is sin, and sin is damnation. Thou art in a parlous state,
shepherd.

CORIN Not a whit, Touchstone. Those that are good manners at the court are as
ridiculous in the country as the behaviour of the country is most mockable at the
court. You told me you salute not at the court, but you kiss your hands: that
courtesy would be uncleanly if courtiers were shepherds. (3.2.40–51)

The interaction of their backgrounds serves as an education for the two
lovers. Although Rosalind mocks the uneducated Orlando's verses – 'Some
of them had in them more feet than the verses would bear' – she learns much
from his simple faith and sincerity, after she has abused them. He in turn
learns sophistication from her. He grows up, and he grows out of games.
This contrast, indeed conflict, was echoed in the design. Farrah startlingly
offset the beauty of the multicoloured forest with a monochromatic court.
The court scenes were set on a white floor with white walls and steel bars,
with actors in black velvet Jacobean-type costumes. On the other hand, the
forest scenes were on a raised stage, rather like a log raft, out of which grew
pines that soared to the heavens, and as spring moved into summer so the
foliage appeared to grow and adorn the stage. The set often reminded me of
scenes I had imagined when reading *Lord of the Rings*.

Opening a play is always difficult. In *As You Like It*, as in many of
Shakespeare's plays, the action starts in the middle of a conversation, but
in this instance Orlando's speech takes on the form of a prologue. We
decided it was to this that Rosalind refers at the end of the play: 'It is not the
fashion to see the lady the epilogue; but it is no more unhandsome to see the
lord the prologue.' So Terry put Adam down-centre on an upturned
bucket and I delivered the exposition through him to the audience. In
rehearsals and early performances this was delivered at breakneck speed.
Like an egg Orlando is hatching, and his rebellion is the outburst of the
prologue in which he justifies to himself his feelings of frustration and
injury. Wise old Adam can only observe for the moment. The play starts at
a climactic point in Orlando's life, a fine vehicle for gripping an audience;
hence the fast, pressured delivery. Later in the run of the play we

compromised a little and I slowed my speech down without, I hope, losing any of the pressure.

The wrestling scene was vital to the production and to my character. Losing weight and visiting a gym three times a week paid dividends. Ian McKay was the fight arranger. I had worked with him before, which meant he knew my limitations. Terry Wood was a marvellous Charles, the wrestler – six feet five inches and approximately twenty stone. I have nightmares about facing lunatic actors in stage fights, but Terry Wood dispelled any fears and I hope I did the same for him. Right from the start there was total trust, always the emphasis was on taking care of each other, and as a result of all this Ian was able to devise a fight that was both spectacularly entertaining and apparently dangerous; so much more diffi-cult to do in unarmed combat than it is with weapons. This proved to be essential to the production. In keeping with the fairy tale idea we had a fight that was reminiscent of professional wrestling at the local town hall between opponents grossly mismatched. It had moments of hilarity mixed with moments of alarming brutality. It was generally at this point that audiences loosened up and sometimes joined in. There were often boos, cheers and rounds of applause. At my suggestion we incorporated a move in which I was hurled headlong into the front row of the audience. This often took me out of the vision of the upper circles and invariably brought them all to their feet, a reaction an actor rarely achieves in a long career. The front row into which I was hurled often produced reactions most actors never see. Old ladies wielding handbags yelled abuse at Charles and pin-stripe-suited stockbroker types bemoaned the fact that, now the leading actor had killed himself, their ticket money and evening out were lost. I am sorry for all the shopping bags and picnic boxes I smashed as I crashed to the feet of the front row, but it was good theatre, and I never met a member of any audience that didn't think it had happened only on their night.

It was this particular move that caused the only serious accident during the run at Stratford. In a performance just before Christmas I had a bad fall. I was on my way into the front row and I landed right on the point of my right shoulder, separating my acromio-clavicular joint. I love the sound of that part of my anatomy, verbal, not actual. I slumped to the floor at the feet of the front row, and lay there grimacing. Occasionally a member of the audience would help me back on to the stage, but not this time. I assumed I had broken something in my shoulder, and decided the best thing to do was to stay there. Charles, my opponent, had other ideas. To my utter horror Terry Wood appeared over the edge of the stage and bent down to help me up. In the true spirit of the theatre yours truly scrambled to his feet and managed one more desperate flying drop-kick before Duke Frederick, appreciating the agony I was in, mercifully came out with the words, 'No more, no more.' But there was more. Having scraped through the rest of the scene, I left the stage to be greeted by the Company Manager, Nick Jones, who had miraculously found a doctor in what seemed like seconds. If I thought the pain I was already suffering was bad, this doctor was about to prove me wrong. Out of earshot of the audience and the other actors a needle the size of a knitting needle was plunged into my shoulder and waggled about until it found the appropriate cavity, where it delivered its painkiller. The relief was instantaneous, and although it began to wear off after an hour or so, it got me through the show. But I shall never forget that needle, and Nick Jones will never forget the agony it caused me. So I was out of the show for a couple of months. I remember one amusing incident. I was walking my dog around the gardens by the theatre one day, my arm in a sling, when I bumped into another member of the company, David Suchet, and another actor, Bernard Lloyd. After talking together for a few minutes it occurred to David that here were three actors, each of whom had played the part of Orlando, and each of whom had suffered in playing it, Bernard with his back and David, like me, with his shoulder. But my injury was simply the result of a stupid mistake. I hadn't been concentrating, I wasn't prepared and I fell incorrectly. There was only myself to blame.

A main character and influence in the story of Orlando is Adam. Although he has reached the seventh age of man, he is the 'venerable' Adam. He is the one who is closest to Orlando throughout the first half of the play. He is the one who warns Orlando of Oliver's murderous intentions. He is the one who suggests Orlando should run away. He even gives Orlando all his savings. It is a truly sympathetic part, and one they say that Shakespeare played himself. In our production Adam was played by Jimmy Gardner, a great friend and a warm and generous man.

Returning home from the wrestling I was confronted with this tiny old man loaded down with several pieces of luggage and a huge two-handed sword. Terry suggested that this sword had been handed down to Adam. Rusty and blunt, it was the only weapon the old man could lay his hands on, but one he could hardly lift. Adam was discovered like this at the beginning of the scene, marching up and down like a sentry on duty, waiting for his master to come home. When we next appeared, in our first forest scene, I, of course, was carrying the sword, all the luggage, and, by

12 'I can live no longer by thinking'

the end of the scene, old Adam as well. I asked Terry if I could use the sword to smash my way into the forest lords' camp, and he agreed. I felt that Orlando was surrounded by enemies at court and here in an alien world his initial and now in-bred reaction was offensive. The stronger the violation of the foresters' camp the greater his surprise when they offer charity and the more poignant his lesson. In response to their gentleness and offers of succour he can think only of Adam, in many ways his saviour, and he rushes off to fetch him. Terry wanted to make the most of the juxtaposition of 'Sans teeth, sans eyes, sans taste, sans everything' with Adam's entrance, so he had me carry Adam like a baby in my arms, and we arrived bang on the end of the line right next to Jaques.

Both Rosalind and Orlando had arrived safely in the forest, and here Terry wanted to end the first half. During the singing of 'Blow, blow, thou winter wind' (another stunning arrangement by Guy Woolfenden) I fondled and kissed the necklace given me by Rosalind after the wrestling – a little touch to relate the two lovers and to put into the audience's mind the prospect of their meeting.

After the interval our fairy tale blossomed, as did our forest set, as indeed did the relationship between Orlando and Rosalind, in the guise of Ganymede, played by Susan Fleetwood. I was often asked if Orlando realized that it was Rosalind with whom he was playing in the forest. It never crossed my mind once. I had only seen her briefly at the wrestling, and although I fell in love with her, trying to recall her face was not easy. Certainly there was a resemblance, and I talk of it to the Duke, her father:

> My lord, the first time that I ever saw him,
> Methought he was a brother to your daughter. (5.4.28–9)

But to mark that would only have been a distraction in the scenes between Rosalind and Orlando in our second half. Orlando is overflowing with love. He bounces on, swirling about the stage, carving up the trees and advertising his love by hanging his terrible poems on every available branch. He is infatuated with the memory of a girl he only saw for a few minutes when he was fighting for his life in the wrestling match.

Terry's simple solution to lovers' games was circles: histories and tragedies have straight lines, comedies and romances have circles. If you had a map of our footprints in the two major scenes of the second half, you would have a picture of spirals all over the stage. And so the first antagonistic contest of a meeting between Orlando and Rosalind swirls and whirls to a feverish climax and an exhausted collapse at the foot of a tree, where Rosalind professes she can cure Orlando of his love by pretending to be his love. Being a gambler at heart I could always appreciate Orlando's willingness to accept this dare. After all, he has nothing to lose. He doesn't think for a moment that this boy can cure him of his love, but these games may pleasingly pass the time.

It transpires that time is of the essence to Rosalind as she complains of Orlando's late arrival into their second forest scene. In our production the preceding Jaques–Rosalind scene was played as a seduction by the melancholic intellectual of the vibrant youth (perhaps in an effort to complement his personality). So at the moment Orlando enters, Ganymede is on the verge of being devoured by Jaques and his cloak. No wonder she reprimands him. For me there was a definite shape to this, the second of the forest scenes. The games reach a crescendo when Rosalind gets Celia to marry them. 'I take thee Rosalind for wife', says Orlando in play and almost collapses in grief, as the despair of his unrequited love looms in his face. He looks at Ganymede and sees Rosalind. This happens again at the end of the scene. Rosalind encourages pretend bed-games based on their discussion of fidelity, and as Orlando makes to go, she rises and, pretending that she is naked, drops Celia's shawl, which they have been using as a bedspread. Orlando is so involved in the game, he almost imagines he sees his love's body. This is too much, the games must cease and he must leave, but Rosalind torments him and makes him promise to return at two o'clock, which he does, 'With no less religion than if thou wert indeed my Rosalind'. He has been wounded deeply, and the next time they meet he has been wounded physically. Rosalind is cruel and he counters her curtly. She goads him and teases him about his love until he can bear it no longer: 'I can live no longer by thinking.' We all felt that it was at this point that Rosalind and Orlando learn their greatest lesson. He realizes that the dream is no substitute for the reality, and she realizes that she has been very wrong to play with Orlando's emotions. Together with Phoebe and Silvius they (Orlando unknowingly) intone their devotion to each other in the quartet at the end of Act 5, Scene 3. Terry tended to leave this scene alone, hoping that when we had become familiar with the lines, we would naturally catch each other's tune as we said the lines. When this happened it made it easy for me to break down on 'To her that is not here, nor doth not hear'.

And so with the stage adorned with colourful blossom and foliage a cart appears, pulled by the forest lords, chariot-style. On board are Corin, commandeered to play Hymen in this pageant (with terrible verse sup-

plied), Celia and Rosalind, dressed as a girl again. All is resolved and all
presumably live happily ever after, as in all fairy tales. To celebrate, the
cast dance and sing. It's a sort of fertility dance, rather like a Morris dance
on the local village green, the audience clap to the beat and finally Rosalind
delivers her epilogue to a sea of smiling, happy faces. I think they've had a
good time.

I hope this has given a taste of the production, how we worked on it and
how we reached various decisions and attitudes to scenes. I cannot
remember enjoying a production so much. Even when I was depressed,
after a few scenes the depression would lift. I believe Terry Hands's

13 'Then is there mirth in heaven'

concept for the piece was excellent, and it was this more than anything that bound the company together and made the work so enjoyable. The production had so much panache and vigour, it was irresistibly entertaining. Entertainment was the key word. I hope Orlando provided a little of it.

Lavatch in
All's Well That Ends Well
GEOFFREY HUTCHINGS

GEOFFREY HUTCHINGS is an Associate Artist of the Royal Shakespeare Company. He joined the Company in 1968, after considerable acting experience both in repertory and in London. He has worked in radio and television, and has also undertaken a United States tour under the auspices of 'Actors in Residence'. At Stratford, his range has covered parts of many types and periods, but he is perhaps best known for his performances, from 1969 onwards, of Shakespeare's clowns: the Young Shepherd in *The Winter's Tale*, Dromio of Syracuse, the Clown in *Antony and Cleopatra*, Feste, Autolycus, Bottom and Launce. He first played Lavatch, with Peggy Ashcroft as the Countess, in the 1981 production of *All's Well That Ends Well*, designed by John Gunter and directed by Trevor Nunn.

In 1926 fire almost totally destroyed the Shakespeare Memorial Theatre at Stratford-upon-Avon. George Bernard Shaw sent a congratulatory telegram. The part left standing and incorporated into the new building is now used as a rehearsal room and is known as the Conference Hall. In 1979 the Royal Shakespeare Company had plans to convert this space into an intimate theatre for the performance of relatively rarely seen Shakespeare plays and other Elizabethan and Jacobean plays. The inaugural production was to be *All's Well That Ends Well*, directed by Trevor Nunn with Judi Dench as Helena and Dame Peggy Ashcroft as the Countess. I was asked to play Lavatch. £250,000 was needed for the initial conversion. On two or three occasions security of the sum seemed possible. One eccentric elderly millionairess offered the whole amount, provided the opening production was *Hamlet* – and that she could play Ophelia. In the end, the money was not forthcoming, the plan was shelved and the production cancelled.

In 1981, I was invited to rejoin the Company to play Lavatch in a production of *All's Well* destined for the main auditorium, directed by

14 'She is not well, but yet she has her health'
Geoffrey Hutchings as Lavatch and Harriet Walter as Helena, November 1981

Trevor Nunn and, by great good fortune, with Dame Peggy as the Countess. I had just finished the previous season in London, playing Feste, and was to start this season with Autolycus, followed by Bottom in *A Midsummer Night's Dream*, the Clown in *Titus Andronicus*, Launce, and ending with Lavatch. My early glances at the plays and the parts confirmed a vague suspicion that Lavatch was going to be the real challenge of the season.

During his initial, introductory talk to the Company about *All's Well*, Trevor Nunn described the reasons why he had wanted to do that particular play in the converted Conference Hall Theatre, had it come into being. He believed it was probably originally performed not at the open-air Globe Theatre but at an indoor theatre, much smaller, not far from the site of the RSC's new London home at the Barbican. He saw it as an intimate 'chamber' piece. The language is conversational rather than declamatory or rhetorical, and there is a finely-woven and rich subtext making comparisons with Tchekov obvious and frequent. These, then, were the reasons for wanting to do that play in that space.

However, we were now to do it in the sixteen-hundred-seat main auditorium. One thing that most literary critics and students of Shakespeare agree on is that *All's Well* is not one of his most popular plays nor his most successful. One scholar goes so far as to suggest that it was written when the author was not in full possession of his faculties. The theatre history of the play has been chequered, to say the least. There had only been two productions of the play, prior to this one, by the RSC, in the past twenty-five years. It is described as a dark comedy, a problem play, but Nunn saw in it a quality of redemption, love and joy which because of its lack of exposure is seldom seen on stage. His intention was that it should be a bitter-sweet celebration of joy and hope. As rehearsals progressed we read the play aloud, scene by scene, analysing the text and discussing the narrative and the action. It became abundantly clear from the start that most people, some greatly experienced in working with Shakespeare texts, were having basic difficulties in understanding what they were reading and therefore in conveying the meaning to others equally bemused. However, thanks to annotated editions of the play, some painstakingly long discussions about differences of interpretation and, above all, the guidance of our skilful and articulate director, we arrived at a level of comprehension which, on rereading, made the scenes so clear that we wondered why initially we had thought them so difficult. This is the fascinating thing about the text of *All's Well*. It is dense. It is complex and convoluted, but

79

once understanding has been achieved, it is so well constructed that it acquires a naturalness and almost modern conversational quality that is not apparent at first. It is also rich in variety.

The first scene opens with 'high' prose, a discussion of the merits of Helena and her father, Gerard de Narbonne, the King's illness and the passing away of the Count of Rossillion; a sensitive prelude to the Countess's farewell to and blessing of Bertram which is in irregular, halting blank verse, in close keeping with the emotion of a mother saying farewell to her only son. After a brief exchange in prose, Helena has her first soliloquy. She knows what she is feeling, there is no uncertainty, and this is reflected in the strong regular verse. Parolles enters and the scene reverts to prose, but of a far less stilted style than that at the opening of the scene. Here are two equals, both from 'below stairs', talking together, and although Helena speaks verse for a dozen lines, the scene continues in conversational prose, until she is left alone for her final soliloquy, which is in regular verse echoing her resolve to go to Paris after Bertram.

Shakespeare uses the variants of prose and verse at his disposal to change and match the mood of the scene. It was from this dense and complicated text, that I had to glean something of the character that I was eventually to portray. The work of an actor on a text is like that of a detective. You have to look for clues to the character's behaviour in what he says, to a certain extent in what others say about him, in what he does and the way in which others react to him. You then have to interpret those clues and bits of information and create in your mind an 'identikit' picture, which is then processed through your senses. Using your own experience, talent and ability, you hope to arrive at a comprehensible and recognizable human being as near as possible to the dramatist's original intentions.

There are essentially three types of Shakespearean clown. First, the Clown himself, whose origins are found in Spanish drama of the sixteenth century in the character of the 'bobo' (cf. booby). He is the archetypal village idiot, the simpleton, epitomized by the character of Peter Simple in *The Merry Wives of Windsor*. The Clown or Young Shepherd in *The Winter's Tale* also displays similar characteristics. Second, the Servant, typified by the Dromios in *The Comedy of Errors* and Launce and Speed in *The Two Gentlemen of Verona*. Having a particular job or function which they perform reasonably competently, their value is enhanced by their wit and humour but their livelihood does not depend upon these skills. Finally, the Fool, the professional jester, who earns his living and maintains his position in the court or household by singing, jesting, mocking and entertaining. Of these there are only four in the whole canon: Feste, Touchstone, the Fool in *King Lear* and Yorick.

I fought hard to convince myself and others that Lavatch fell into this last category. The Countess says of him, that the late Count, her husband, 'made himself much sport out of him; by his authority he remains here, which he thinks is a patent for his sauciness; and indeed he has no pace, but runs where he will' (4.5.64–7).

This readiness to exceed the licence afforded them was common among professional jesters. Indeed, the opening scene between the Countess and Lavatch is strongly reminiscent of Feste's first encounter with Olivia in *Twelfth Night*. In both, the fools avoid severe reprimand by making light of the situation and joking. Remember, too, that Feste had been originally employed by the late head of the household; he was 'a fool the Lady Olivia's father took much delight in'. What offences have been committed by the two characters are unknown but with skill and dexterity they avoid the wrath and censure of their respective employers.

What does Lavatch himself imply when asked directly by Lafew?

LAFEW   Whether dost thou profess thyself – a knave or a fool?
CLOWN   A fool, sir, at a woman's service, and a knave at a man's.
LAFEW   Your distinction?
CLOWN   I would cozen the man of his wife, and do his service.
LAFEW   So you were a knave at his service indeed.
CLOWN   And I would give his wife my bauble, sir, to do her service.
LAFEW   I will subscribe for thee; thou art both knave and fool.   (4.5.22–32)

Despite my original thoughts, more and more evidence of this kind suggested that he was in fact a combination of Clown and Servant, fulfilling some unspecified function at Rossillion, but having the licence to speak his mind in a witty and often outspoken way. Dame Peggy believed that he was the illegitimate son of the Count and a cook they once had. However, we do know that his roots are more likely to be rural than urban. The language he uses suggests a life spent on the land.

He that ears my land spares my team and gives me leave to in the crop.   (1.3.44–5)

I am a woodland fellow, sir, that always loved a great fire.   (4.5.47–8)

The word Clown ought to give us a clue but does not give us the whole answer. Throughout the play he is called 'a witty fool', 'sir knave', 'your worship', 'sirrah' (three times), 'sir' (five times), 'knave' (eight times), and finally, in the last scene with Parolles, and the only time in the play that he is referred to by name, 'Good Master Lavatch'. The name itself is often a good clue to Shakespeare's characters. There are rural connections both in the French (*la vache*) and in the anglicized version. I live in Stroud in Gloucestershire and across the Slad valley from my house is a small collection of houses called the Vatch. I discovered, from research in the local library, that on the site once stood a mill which was used for the storing and processing of animal fodder from vetch, a plant of the pea family used, wild or cultivated, for forage. Lavatch's domicile at Rossillion in provincial France suggests country roots, and his attitude to the court and all that it stands for is seen in the following exchange with the Countess:

CLOWN   I know my business is but to the court.
COUNTESS   To the court! Why, what place make you special, when you put off that with such contempt? But to the court!
CLOWN   Truly madam, if God have lent a man any manners he may easily put it off at court: he that cannot make a leg, put off's cap, kiss his hand, and say nothing, has neither leg, hands, lip, nor cap; and indeed such a fellow, to say precisely, were not for the court.   (2.2.4–13)

Incidentally, I wonder if the Elizabethan audience was quicker than our modern day audiences to pick up on this marvellous piece of 'sick' humour? The language is obscure to our ears, but the idea of a lipless, handless, legless person not really being suitable for court strikes me as high-quality black comedy.

Lavatch's contempt for the court is also shown when he describes the courtiers that have arrived at Rossillion with Bertram: 'Faith, there's a dozen of 'em with delicate fine hats and most courteous feathers which bow the head and nod at every man' (4.5.104–6). We also know that he is in service:

Service is no heritage, and I think I shall never have the blessing of God till I have issue a' my body; for they say barnes are blessings.   (1.3.23–6)

That man should be at woman's command, and yet no hurt done!   (1.3.93–3)

Many a man's tongue shakes out his master's undoing.   (2.4.23–4)

And Lafew directs him to let his horses be well looked to (4.5.58).

So having read aloud through four acts of the play, with discussion, I knew that Lavatch was rustic rather than urban, and was more likely to be primarily a servant rather than a professional fool. At this point in rehearsal Dickensian commitments took Trevor Nunn to Broadway for ten days. Just before leaving, he revealed his plans for the setting and historical context of the production.

There is a strong military presence in the play and to set it in Elizabethan times presents the problem of finding a recognizable and consistent design for the uniforms. To update the play too much would not be totally successful either. In our sophisticated world of nuclear and anti-nuclear warfare there is little room for the attitude displayed by the young bucks at the court of France, longing to prove themselves and seeing the battlefield as the ideal opportunity for them to win their spurs. The optimum historical setting seemed to be 1910, the *Belle Epoque*: Europe just after the turn of the century and just prior to the first major world confrontation. The importance of class in the play and the emergence of women in society were both helped by this choice. The set, designed by John Gunter, and the costumes by Lindy Hemming were spectacular, rich and extravagant, underlining Trevor Nunn's resolve to make the play work well in a larger space than that for which he had originally intended it.

Cicely Berry, the RSC's Director of Voice, had been taking regular classes with the Company in work connected with the play, reading and studying the metaphysical poets and looking at poems about war. In Trevor's absence we were left in her care and under her expert guidance. We continued to finish the reading and discussion work and then worked through the scenes in smaller groups, experimenting and trying them in various different ways. Dame Peggy had not yet joined the Company from Canada and another actress, Juliette Mole, very kindly volunteered to read the part of the Countess, and we had some exciting and lively sessions experimenting with the scenes – from rolling over and over on the floor (no mean feat reading a text at the same time!) to doing a scene with the Countess seated on my lap. The purpose of these exercises was to free the actor from any automatic or preconceived responses to the text and it brought to light important character attitudes which had nothing necessarily to do with the way in which we were doing the exercise. The one thing which was becoming more and more clear was the importance of the relationship between the Countess and Lavatch. A relationship which went beyond that of a mistress and her servant, a very deep understanding and love of the one for the other, which makes nonsense of Tyrone Guthrie's cutting the part of Lavatch totally from his 1959 production at Stratford-upon-Avon.

All through this initial period I was working without an accent. The choice of the right accent for a character is difficult. It's easy to do an accent, any accent, and then justify the reason for using it; but to find the right accent you must first know the character and be sure that the accent you choose fits that knowledge. Already this season I was using a London (Cockney) accent for Autolycus, a Northern (Leeds) accent for Bottom and a West Country accent for the Clown in *Titus* and Launce in *The Two Gentlemen of Verona*. I suspected, erroneously, that I should find a new accent for Lavatch. The error of my thinking lay in the fact that Lavatch is himself and not any other character, and it would be perfectly possible and right to play four different characters in the same accent (provided that it fitted each character) but still make them different. After all, my physical appearance is the same in all the other productions. I eventually decided to use my own original accent, South Dorset.

Where did the updating of the piece leave me? I had to find a modern function for the character that would allow him to behave in the way that he does. One of the recurrent topics of his conversation is religion; there are more than a dozen references to the Bible and the clergy:

> I'm no great Nabuchadnezzar, sir; I have not much skill in grass.   (4.5.20–1)

> I am for the house with the narrow gate.   (4.5.50–1)

Some are mocking or scurrilous:

> One, that she's not in heaven, whither God send her quickly! The other, that she's in earth, from whence God send her quickly!   (2.4.11–13)

> young Charbon the puritan and old Poysam the papist.   (1.3.51–2)

> as the nun's lip to the friar's mouth.   (2.2.26–7)

But others have a certain weight:

> I think I shall never have the blessing of God till I have issue a' my body.   (1.3.24–5)

> I have been, madam, a wicked creature, as you and all flesh and blood are, and indeed I do marry that I may repent.   (1.3.35–7)

There seems to be within him a continual battle between the forces of good and evil. His general level of thought and reference is very crude and low, resorting continually to very basic bawdy and sexual humour. Nevertheless, through this there shine occasional moments of enlightenment, displaying a spiritual maturity belied by his normal behaviour. It was wondering about this internal conflict that led me to what was probably the most important decision in my development of the character. I had toyed with the idea of making him a defrocked priest. Sir Peter Hall expounds a theory in which he endeavours to find a link between Shakespearean clowns by proving them to have had training for holy orders and for some reason not to have followed their vocation. I couldn't find sufficient justification here for doing that.

I began, though, to think about other ways of setting him apart, and wondered if he should be in some degree physically abnormal. The history of professional fools is full of references to dwarfs and hunchbacks being used as a butt, a figure of fun and, in time, they developed a reputation and skill in providing their patrons with a constant and ready source of wit and invective. When confronted by some physical deformity it is natural for most people who believe themselves to be normal to extend towards that person an element of generosity and licence that would not be granted to a so-called equal. This would allow Lavatch the freedom to express himself without fear of censure.

When I next met Trevor, he too had thought that we might experiment with some physical disability. May I point out at this stage that the only conclusion drawn was that 'there might be something physically wrong with him'. The next day I was called to the wardrobe for a fitting. When I arrived, mystified, for no fittings had been arranged for other members of the cast, I enquired as to the purpose of my privileged summons. 'Oh', they said, as if they fitted them to all actors as a matter of course, 'It's for your hump!' In rehearsal, the following week, I experimented. I launched boldly into a character whose shambling gait and incoherent diction made Quasimodo seem like the Queen Mother. This became eventually modified into a recognizable human being as I began to draw on sense-memories. As a boy in Dorset, I often used to see a farmer taking his milk churns from his farm on a cart: a small figure with a stick, walking by his horse, his back bent and his legs bowed with age and labour. I remember from his knees to his boots he wore very shiny leather gaiters. Other such memories of people I had known or seen helped me to establish a kinesthetic picture in my mind of how the character moved and felt. I have been asked if the germ for the idea of making him a 'hunchback' had come from his line on leaving for the court, 'I am there before my legs.' I can only say that it did not. Such was the organic growth of the character that I hadn't perceived this as being funny in that way until I actually did it before an audience. I'd thought it a witty line purely in terms of its word-play and not connected with his physical appearance.

As I have hinted, the most important relationship for him is that with the Countess. She says that he is tolerated because the late Count was so fond of him and enjoyed his company, but there is an underlying, unspoken respect which she herself extends to him which almost approaches a need.

She tolerates his quips and his vulgarity, and encouraged by his foolery is eventually persuaded to join in. 'To be young again, if we could, I will be a fool in question, hoping to be the wiser by your answer' (2.2.38–9). Like the younger Countess in *Twelfth Night* 'for want of other idleness' she 'bides his proof'. This is a vital scene in the development and understanding of the relationship. It is the only scene that Shakespeare writes for just the two characters and it is essential to see why he has done this. It is a short scene, some 65 lines long; but it could have been shorter. After all, Lavatch is going to Paris to deliver a letter, nothing more. Why is *he* going? The Countess has just buried her husband; first her son and then her favourite gentlewoman have left her. Her household is dwindling; presumably there is no one else. But why is the scene the length it is? What does it tell us? Apart from developing Lavatch's repertoire of jokes, it shows us two people enjoying each other's company and, by implication, suggests strongly that they are both delaying the moment of separation. The Countess's final 'Haste you again' is a cry of loneliness and sadness.

This brings into question the sincerity or levity of his initial request (1.3)

15 'You understand me?'
Lavatch and the Countess (Peggy Ashcroft)

to leave her service. I think he asks to leave in order to prevent the possibility of being dismissed. Although she says 'I'll talk with you more anon', the subject is never referred to again.

It also brings us to the question of the reality or otherwise of Isbel, the woman. In this production, she exists and appears on stage, pursued by Lavatch in the scene-change that precedes 1.1 and, again, rejected by him, in the change prior to 5.5. This obviously works visually and is a help to the audience, but I have an unreasonable suspicion that she only exists in the mind of the Countess and Lavatch. She is part of some verbal game of sexual jealousy that they play together. He alludes to her only twice, once at the beginning: 'If I may have your ladyship's good will to go to the world, Isbel the woman and I will do as we may' (1.3.17–19), and again on his return from the court:

I have no mind to Isbel since I was at court. Our old ling and our Isbels a' th' country are nothing like your old ling and your Isbels a' th' court. The brains of my Cupid's knock'd out, and I begin to love as an old man loves money, with no stomach. (3.2.12–16)

I feel that if the relationship was really important the character would be written into a scene or, at least, she would be referred to by another character. It is similar in feel to, but not entirely the same as, Dromio of Syracuse's experience with Nell, the kitchen wench in *The Comedy of Errors*. There the off-stage meeting only serves as a springboard for one marvellously funny scene between servant and master. This is not the case with Isbel; whether the character exists or not is unimportant, but I think the real reason for references made to her is muddled if she is actually included on stage in the action. Isbel is there, I think, to show Lavatch's attitude towards women and to enrich his relationship with the Countess.

His reason for marriage is partly founded on lust: 'My poor body, madam, requires it; I am driven on by the flesh and he must needs go that the devil drives' (1.3.28–30). He encourages unfaithfulness in a wife, hoping that this infidelity will provide him with children:

The knaves come to do that for me which I am aweary of. He that ears my land spares my team and gives me leave to in the crop; if I be his cuckold, he's my drudge. He that comforts my wife is the cherisher of my flesh and blood; he that cherishes my flesh and blood loves my flesh and blood; he that loves my flesh and blood is my friend; ergo, he that kisses my wife is my friend. If men could be contented to be what they are there were no fear in marriage. (1.3.43–51)

He sees the state of cuckoldry as acceptable and inevitable:

> Your marriage comes by destiny;
> Your cuckoo sings by kind. (1.3.62–3)

87

But he believes it no easy task to find a good woman;

And we might have a good woman born but or every blazing star or at an earthquake, 'twould mend the lottery well; a man may draw his heart out ere 'a pluck one.

(1.3.86–9)

And he corrupts a popular song of the day to prove his point.

There is one other peculiarity which relates to his dealings with the Countess. He seems to prepare her for what is going to happen. Not necessarily in a clairvoyant way but as some sort of protective measure. On several occasions he attempts to lessen the blow of news of events which are likely to disturb her. He interrupts the conversation between her and Reynaldo (1.3) before the steward has time to get to the crux of his speech, namely that he believes Helena to be in love with Bertram; Lavatch proceeds to talk about marriage and infidelity and, when asked to fetch Helena, recites a verse about the paucity of good women. On his return from court, he intimates that all is not well with Bertram. Seconds later, the Countess receives news that her son has run away to the wars. The strongest moment of their mutual bond is possibly in the last scene they have together (4.5). In this scene they have no exchanges at all. Lavatch talks with Lafew but not with the Countess, and even at the end of the scene, when he announces Bertram's return, she does not reply. The understanding they have of each other makes words unnecessary.

I must try to put into words the feeling of privilege and pleasure I have experienced from working with Dame Peggy Ashcroft. Her continually probing mind during rehearsals, her willingness to experiment, her total unselfishness and the dignity, radiance and economy which she brings on stage is a joy to share. She has the freshness and flexibility of approach to each performance that are a lesson to any actor.

Of Lavatch's other relationships in the play – he obviously likes Helena. When they believe her dead, he provides a touching and fitting epitaph:

She was the sweet-marjoram of the sallet, or rather, the herb of grace. (4.5.16–17)

He encounters only two other people in the course of the action: Parolles and Lafew. Both he exposes, Parolles for being a pretender to what he is not:

To say nothing, to do nothing, to know nothing and to have nothing, is to be a great part of your title, which is within a very little of nothing.　(2.4.24–7)

And he seems to hint at what will happen eventually to Parolles: 'many a man's tongue shakes out his master's undoing' (2.4.23–4). The other, the

Lord Lafew, he condemns for being a courtier, implying that as such he is beyond salvation:

let his [the devil's] nobility remain in's court, I am for the house with the narrow gate, which I take to be too little for pomp to enter; some that humble themselves may, but the many will be too chill and tender, and they'll be for the flow'ry way that leads to the broad gate and the great fire. (4.5.49–55)

Some critics have suggested that Lafew thinks little of Lavatch and is unperturbed by him. Robert Eddison who played Lafew in this production responded beautifully to the searing look I gave him at the end of that speech, and was obviously unsettled by the experience. He describes Lavatch just after this as 'A shrewd knave and an unhappy' (4.5.63), possibly the most accurate description of the character.

Having created the character, discovered his attitudes to life, found the logic behind his thinking, his motivations and drives, it doesn't seem to me difficult to make the humour work, particularly with such a superb writer of comedy as Shakespeare. The wit of his first exchange with the Countess, 'No, madam, 'tis not so well that I am poor', leaves the audience in no doubt from the outset as to their expected relationship with the character. The keen sense of rhythm and timing found in his writing of 'jokes' makes them easy to play even if the exact meaning of half the words is not understood by the modern audience. The sequence of thought processes leading from 'He that ears my land spares my team and gives me leave to in the crop' to the culminative 'ergo, he that kisses my wife is my friend' is perfect comic structure. The audience is led skilfully through a tapestry of explanation to a succinct and sure-fire punch line. Audiences love vulgarity and laugh at it, particularly when it is introduced so unexpectedly as 'the barber's chair that fits all buttocks'. They also like a character who is outspoken and cheeky, whether the attack is harmless or incisive.

I was apprehensive of the 'Oh, Lord!' sequence and on the page it is not easy to see how it could be funny. However, when acted out, the scene immediately comes to life. The willingness of the Countess to involve herself, the skill with which both she and Lavatch invent and react to the variations and the final defeat of Lavatch by the Countess at his own game, are, at once, charming, witty, funny and touching. The business of Parolles 'smelling of Fortune's strong displeasure' is brilliantly wittily written and my reaction to his state was heightened by seeking fragrance from a rosebud that I wore in my buttonhole, rather like Cardinal Wolsey sniffing at his pomander.

I have taken a little licence of my own. I'm sure that the reference to 'jade's tricks' would have evoked some response from an Elizabethan audience which is totally lost today. During the scene prior to this exit line I busied myself, discreetly, in sweeping leaves into a neat and prominent pile at the back of the stage. At the end of the sequence 'own rights by the law of nature' I destroyed the pile with one anarchic sweep of my broom as I went off. This physical gesture provided a laugh at exactly the point where Shakespeare intended it to be elicited verbally.

POSTSCRIPT   During the performance of *All's Well*, bent double as I was, I experienced no physical discomfort whatsoever. But I got the most awful back-ache typing out my thoughts on Lavatch.

Nurse in
Romeo and Juliet

BRENDA BRUCE

B RENDA BRUCE, an Associate Artist of the Royal Shakespeare Company, has been with the Company since 1964. Her acting experience has been in every sense extensive. She has appeared in theatres all over the world (including South America and China), in films, and on television, where her performance in *The Winter's Tale* won her the Best Actress Evening Standard Award. At Stratford, she has played at both The Other Place and the Royal Shakespeare Theatre, where her range has covered Mistress Page, Paulina, Maria in *Twelfth Night*, Gertrude, Lady Capulet and Mistress Quickly in *Henry V*. She first played the Nurse in the *Romeo and Juliet* production of 1980, repeating her performance in the 1981 seasons at Newcastle and the Aldwych. With her were Anton Lesser as Romeo and Judy Buxton as Juliet, and the production, designed by Ralph Koltai, was directed by Ron Daniels.

Nurse is one of those *famous* roles in Shakespeare. The theatrical history books are full of references to the brilliance of revered actresses, each seemingly 'definitive'. Some of them Dames! If Nurse was a part played by Dame Edith Evans and Ellen Terry and Mrs Stirling and Beatrix Lehmann and Celia Johnson, to name but a few, who was I to waver at the chance? I had always felt that if I played Nurse whilst I was still young enough I would take as starting-point her lines from her first speech, referring to her own baby Susan. 'Susan and she [Juliet] were of an age. Well, Susan is with God, she was too good for me.' If Nurse's baby died eleven years ago and she became Juliet's wet nurse, she could not be older than forty. Later in the same speech, describing her weaning of Juliet, she says to Lady Capulet, 'My Lord and you were then at Mantua.' This suggests that Nurse has been responsible for Juliet's upbringing. She is in fact the Mother, the person in whom Juliet lays her trust and confides her secret love. She sees Paris as the perfect answer to all her hopes for her

16 'There stays a husband to make you a wife'
Brenda Bruce as Nurse with Judy Buxton as Juliet, April 1980

'baby', Juliet – love, marriage, children – simply the woman's lot, which can be pleasurable. Lady Capulet is mainly interested in the social position that will be gained for the Capulets through such a marriage.

In my opinion, Nurse is no country bumpkin. She holds a very important position with an important family in Verona. She is the Italian equivalent of a bright Cockney with all the same energetic vulgarity and warmth, and the only interest in her life is Juliet and Juliet's happiness. A fairly simple premise. However the complications within the part are tremendous. As so often with Shakespeare's major supporting parts, the subtext is very difficult to play. The jokes are obscure:

NURSE Doth not rosemary and Romeo begin both with a letter?
ROMEO Ay, Nurse, what of that? Both with an 'R'.
NURSE Ah, mocker, that's the dog's name. 'R' is for the –   (2.4.206–10)

But Nurse stops herself saying whatever rude word she has in mind. The reference books state, 'Nurse cannot read'! I decided to face that problem with an audience! Along with Maria in *Twelfth Night* and Gertrude in *Hamlet*, Nurse is a reporter. In almost every scene she reports happenings to the other characters, most often repeating what has already been seen by the audience. She nudges Juliet sexually as Mercutio nudges Romeo in the same manner.

I realized that work at home was out of the question. The reaction of Tybalt, Mercutio, Romeo, Juliet and the Capulets and a director who allowed *room* for Nurse's subtext and did not treat her as a garrulous joke was the only way to find a true character. We did not read through the play at the first rehearsal. Nor did we see any designs. The set was a piece of cardboard two feet by one foot with two angled walls that were to move about, plus a bench the size of a matchbox and a bed two inches square. I saw that 'we' were on our own! None of us had ever worked together before. We eyed each other with respect, but gingerly, and plunged in scene by scene. I made some instant coffee for myself and shared it with a glamorous lady who turned out to be the dress designer, Nadine Bayliss. She explained that the boys were in leather, the girls in 1980 up-market hand-knitted silk dresses. 'And Nurse?', I said. 'Oh yes, you too, with an outrageous purple and silver cloak and long glass earrings for the street scene.' Tentatively I suggested red bubble curls for my hair. She would check with Ron Daniels (director). He approved this, so at least I knew how I would appear. If I had found myself weighed down with layers of heavy woollen skirts, my face and head half hidden in a wimple, the feeling of lightness and delight I was hoping to achieve in the first scene would have been a much more difficult task. The first time I played Gertrude in *Hamlet* I was encased in white sheepskin. I felt and looked like a bedside rug. Ron also liked my idea of a young Nurse and so work began.

My first rehearsal work was on Act 3, Scene 2 – Nurse returning with the news of Tybalt's death. Realizing that Juliet had fallen in love with him, she had arranged their marriage; the Capulets, Paris, protocol, meant nothing to her; only Juliet's happiness mattered. If the fight between the households had not taken place, Nurse, I am sure, could have pleaded Romeo and Juliet's case. The first scene of Act 3 was all too familiar in 1981. The children, carrying their elders' bitterness and aggression and bigotry into the streets, fight and kill each other. The audience watch the scene but Nurse must repeat it to Juliet. Although she is not in the scene, she reports Tybalt's death in detail. She cries, 'Tybalt, Tybalt the best friend I had'. Why? She never speaks to Tybalt. We decided that Nurse should arrive at the party in Act 1 with Tybalt, that he and Nurse should lead the dancing and that Nurse should be very aware of the ensuing arguments between Tybalt and Romeo and Tybalt and Capulet. So during the weeks we tried to cope with all our various problems. We began sonnet classes with Terry Hands and Cicely Berry. She is in charge of voice, speech, and the presentation of the text. These sessions were nerve-racking but gradually broke down the barriers between the actors. Generalization was not allowed; we had to be specific; we had to learn to look each other in the eye and *tell* the sonnets to each other. Cicely Berry took speeches at random; we sat in a circle and, starting with the first word, spoke one each, in correct sequence, slowly, halting at first; but gradually one forgot oneself, picked up the word and passed it on to the next actor. We learned to *listen* to the actor on the left and *give* to the actor on the right. With practice it became like a near-perfect relay race; accepting and passing, we became one voice. We began to listen to each other, share with each other, keep Shakespeare's rhythm without falling into meaningless rhetoric, choose words specific to the speech without chopping up the rhythm – difficult at first, but when carried into rehearsal most helpful.

I like to start with a simple outline of character and fill in details as I work with fellow actors, quite often elaborating, then discarding; always trying to keep in mind that the audience will have a great influence on one's performance.

But I determined to tell the story from Nurse's point of view; with every

94

report *tell* the story; no striving for laughs, no stressing of the verbal juggling.

The street scene with Mercutio, Benvolio and Romeo was a 'pig'. There was nothing in the script to suggest what the boys do to Nurse to cause her extreme indignation: 'Now, afore God, I am so vexed that every part about me quivers.' We struggled on, trying to invent outrageous business. We did not solve the scene satisfactorily before the first preview. After weeks before audiences who were patently not very amused, Jonathan Hyde (Mercutio) came into my dressing-room for our nightly two-handed note session, with the answer. I had fallen between two stools. I had not quite thrown off the old Nurse image. I was playing old Nurse taking umbrage. Wrong. The boys were leather-clad, greasy-haired, *menacing*. Wrong. The audience was not prepared to laugh at the ill-treatment of Nurse. It was distasteful. Since by now we knew each other rather well and trusted each other as actors, we agreed to improvise the next night. The boys were light and frivolous and I *enjoyed* their fun. Instead of using my fan to make a ladylike image, I hit them about their heads. It was a Japanese paper fan and made a sharp noise. The audience laughed. After three slaps they laughed and clapped. After a few performances the fan broke and the prop boys substituted another fan. It was short and the ribs were made of plastic, instead of cane. When I hit the boys the smart crack was missing. The wonderful tingle of comedy-timing disappeared. On my free days I drove to all the Japanese emporiums from Oxford to East Finchley in search of the correct fan, without much luck. Comedy is almost impossible to explain. A sharp noise evoked by a quick light slap is very amusing. Hard hitting is *not* so funny. We four went on working with our audiences and the scene grew in sheer fun.

In time we started to rehearse Act 2, Scene 5, Nurse's return from the street scene. My Nurse could not truthfully (and I had to believe in my chosen interpretation) be so utterly exhausted after a trip into town. It had to be Mother saying, 'Let me get in and sit down before you badger me – I'll tell you everything you want so much to know, after a sit down. Wait, calm down, my back aches, my head throbs and I think Romeo is a poor choice.' After some teasing, Nurse with one of her inevitably bawdy comments sends Juliet off to Friar Laurence to be married:

> I am the drudge and toil in your delight
> But you shall bear the burden soon at night. (2.5.75–6)

At the Royal Shakespeare Company we always have *solus* calls. It gives one the chance to work on personal problems without pressure. The time had come to look at Nurse in the scenes up to the marriage of Romeo and Juliet. Nurse's long speech in 1.3 was giving me great trouble. I was very afraid it was boring. Ron pointed out that I was rushing it, not enjoying the language. He told me to *talk* to him. Look him in the eye and *tell* him the story of the weaning of Juliet. We spent an hour on that one speech. It was weeks before I got anywhere near what Ron wanted but in that first hour I began to enjoy the picture of the hot afternoon before the earthquake.

> Sitting in the sun under the dovehouse wall . . .
> And then my husband – God be with his soul!
> 'A was a merry man – took up the child.   (1.3.27, 39–40)

Quite apart from giving an audience information about Nurse, the speech paints a wonderful picture of the domestic life of the Capulets. Technically, the energy must keep right through to the lines:

> Peace, I have done, God mark thee to his Grace,
> Thou wast the prettiest babe that e'er I nursed.
> An I might live to see thee married once
> I have my wish.   (1.3.59–62)

Nurse would be completely fulfilled if Juliet might be 'A happy Mother made'. Juliet *is* Nurse's life. In fact after Juliet's apparent death, Nurse fades out of the play. When Juliet is dead, there is no Nurse.

The work on the first half of the play had reached a point when I must decide on Nurse's basic qualities, her philosophy, character, morality and position with regard to the Capulet family. I made a list of notes for myself. These were to cover the first half of the play; the question of Nurse's morality after the death of Tybalt was yet to come. The philosophy: it is a man's world, it is a young world. Very young girls must prepare for love, especially the physical aspect of love and the inevitable outcome, 'women grow by men'. But she believes in romantic love and happiness and babies; yet she is a religious woman who calls upon God a great deal. Her position in the Capulet family is that of a servant, who once her position as wet nurse is over and Juliet is weaned, is kept in their employ. She teaches Juliet to 'run and waddle about'. She runs the household, she is a 'retainer' and she is Juliet's confidante. She is not, so far, a deep-thinking woman; she has only learned to live with the inevitable happenings of a life such as hers. Her infant dead, her husband dead, she dedicates her life to Juliet. If Juliet really loves Romeo, then Nurse will do everything in her power to see them married. There is nothing to indicate that she has any qualms with regard to the Capulet/Montague feud.

Nurse's bawdiness is part of her character. She cannot resist sexual innuendo. It is a running joke; often after a bawdy remark she says 'May God forgive me.' Her sexual jokes are never intended to be leering or lascivious. I was brought up in a working-class family. The general good-natured innuendo shocked my young romantic feelings. In retrospect I saw it for what it was: a running joke against a woman's lot; a built-in sense of timing; what a music-hall comic would call 'a throw away'. But like the female members of my family, Nurse has a very moral attitude; for instance in 2.4, in one of her speeches to Romeo: 'the gentlewoman is young and therefore, if you should deal double with her, truly it were an ill thing to be offered to any gentlewoman, and very weak dealing' (2.4.167–70). Nurse is as severe in her interviewing of Romeo as a possible suitor as Capulet is in his interviewing of Paris. Of one thing I was certain, I must not shy away from Nurse's bawdiness, neither must I demand audience reaction (some of the references and puns are anyway too obscure). Shakespeare had written a Cockney wit into a Veronese nurse. Until the death of Tybalt Nurse must enjoy every second. As I have said before, but for the death of Tybalt, Romeo and Juliet might have lived happily ever after. Nurse would have pleaded their case and might have won the Capulets over. That is not the story of Romeo and Juliet. Those were my notes to myself for the first half of the play!

We started work on 3.2. Ron, cleverly I think, set the scene in exactly the same way as for Nurse's return from the street scene (2.4, 5), when she was quite knowingly teasing Juliet. 3.1 had been a very different street scene. The jokes are over. We are facing tragedy. Nurse once again talks at cross purposes – not, as I see it, because she is hysterical, but because she is in a state of shock. Mercutio killed, her best friend Tybalt murdered by Romeo, Romeo banished, out of her despair she turns on 'men' with quiet deep bitterness, as though she is discovering the darker side of human relationships for the first time:

> There's no trust,
> No faith, no honesty in men; all perjured,
> All forsworn, all naught, all dissemblers.
> Ah, where's my man? Give me some aqua vitae.   (3.2.85–8)

Here in the speech I took a liberty! I cut 'give me some aqua vitae', using 'Ah, where's my man?' as a cry for my dead husband, someone of my own to help my anguish:

> These griefs, these woes, these sorrows make me old.
> Shame come to Romeo.   (3.2.89–90)

97

Life is not only love, marriage, babies. There is bitterness and loss and waste. Yet once again she cannot resist Juliet. As she takes the desperate child in her arms, she promises to find Romeo and help them consummate their marriage.

Morally how does Nurse stand? Does one protect, in fact encourage one's child to harbour, a convicted murderer? The answer must be yes, if, like Nurse, one believes that happiness with one's chosen man, however fleeting, is the very essence of life. There have been murderers and deserters since the beginning of history who have gained respite because of the loyalty of their women.

In 3.5, Nurse stands silent, horrified as Capulet rages against his daughter. Nurse alone knows that Romeo and Juliet are married. She alone knows the real cause of Juliet's hysterical agony. She speaks once, briefly turning on Capulet:

> God in heaven bless her!
> You are to blame, my lord, to rate her so. (3.5.168–9)

17 'Why should you fall into so deep an O?'
Nurse comforts Romeo (Anton Lesser)

Nurse has until this moment been treated by the Capulets rather as they would treat a poor relation; used, teased and shown a certain aloof kind of affection, but Capulet's reply

> Peace you mumbling fool!
> Utter your gravity o'er a gossip's bowl,
> For here we need it not   (3.5.173–5)

reminds us that Nurse is after all 'only a servant'.

I think the most terrible moment for Nurse is Lady Capulet's withdrawal of all motherly comfort:

> Talk not to me, for I'll not speak a word,
> Do as thou wilt, for I have done with thee.   (3.5.202–3)

Why doesn't Nurse tell the truth and confess her part in the marriage? Out of loyalty to Juliet? Out of some mistaken idea that all may yet be well? Out of the fear of dismissal? Shakespeare gives no indication. When the parents have left the room, Juliet begs Nurse for help:

> What sayest thou? Hast thou not a word of joy?
> Some comfort, Nurse.   (3.5.211–12)

Now came the 'crunch', Nurse's advice to Juliet; I think it best to write the speech in sections and explain my specific decisions. Capulet's anger with Juliet (especially 3.5.176–95) serves as my subtext:

> Graze where you will, you shall not house with me . . .
> An you be mine, I'll give you to my friend,
> An you be not, hang, beg, starve, die in the streets. (3.5.188, 191–2)

Nurse could advise Juliet to run away with her to Friar Laurence, seek refuge in a nunnery, follow Romeo into Mantua, call her mother and father, confess to them, pray for their understanding and forgiveness, and with their help plead with the Prince to forgive Romeo. If any of these solutions had been in Shakespeare's *Romeo and Juliet* the play would be a drama, not a tragedy. As it is, Juliet is unschooled in life – a fourteen-year-old girl – and her closest companion is Nurse, with whom she shares her waking and sleeping hours (in 4.3.10 Juliet refers to Nurse not sharing her room as usual, but sitting up with Lady Capulet). Nurse is incapable of sending Juliet out into the world; Juliet's parents are moreover full of grudge against the Montagues, a 'continuing rage'. Nurse has only one answer and it is immoral and against the law. It is damnation in the eyes of the church, but better than starving on the streets. Her solution is *bigamy*. How to begin to give this advice? I wrote earlier of a director who gives space for subtext. Ron Daniels gave it to me. I've written beside the speech to Juliet, 'Take all the time in the world.' 'Faith, here it is.'

> Romeo is banished; and all the world to nothing
> That he dares ne'er come back to challenge you. (3.5.213–14)

There must be no hint of emotion in the voice, no attempt at physical comfort. Those two lines are a simple statement of fact.

> Then, since the case so stands as now it doth,
> I think it best you married with the County. (3.5.216–17)

Anything is better than family rejection, starvation. There would be nothing for a girl, alone in the world – only begging on the streets. Parental control and approval and marriage were the only possibilities for a woman. Independence for the Juliets of that time was out of the question. As though to soften the shock for Juliet of 'I think it best you married with the County', Nurse says,

> Oh he's a lovely gentleman!
> Romeo's a dishclout to him. (3.5.218–19)

If Nurse sounds as though she believed this, she will get a laugh from the audience. What I wanted was a reaction of shock. When I play well I often get this reaction. I would like the audience to feel let down by someone, whose motives they have trusted. Nurse carries on to the end of the speech with her advice, not believing a word of it, in her heart. Then Juliet asks, 'Speakest thou from thy heart?' And Nurse answers, 'And from my soul too. Else beshrew them both.' In an attempt to make the advice acceptable, Nurse fusses about, making the bed, trying to make everything 'sensible and acceptable'. But Juliet answers, 'Amen' – in other words, 'Devil take you!'

From then on Nurse is watchful; Juliet returns from Friar Laurence's cell, happy, it seems, after her meeting with Paris. Nurse is not certain; she watches her child's reactions. 'See', she says, 'where she comes from shrift with merry look.' Juliet seems merry. She leaves Nurse to choose her wedding-gown – again subtext ('Ay, those attires are best', 4.3.1) – and then:

> I pray thee leave me to myself tonight.
> For I have need of many orisons
> To move the heavens to smile upon my state,
> Which, well thou knowest, is cross and full of sin. (4.3.2–5)

Nurse knows; it was Nurse's advice; she knows Juliet is married, and advised her to commit bigamy. At this moment Shakespeare does not give Nurse any lines. Lady Capulet kisses her child and goes happily to bed. Nurse can only search Juliet's face for a second and scurry off to prepare the wedding-breakfast.

In 4.5 Nurse comes to awaken Juliet. All fears allayed, a conscience stifled; teasing, bawdy Nurse once again. Juliet is dead. Here Shakespeare abandons Nurse. She joins in a formal lament and disappears from the story. In 5.3, the Friar confesses his part in the tragedy and says, 'and to the marriage / Her nurse is privy'. Nurse is not in the scene to put *her* case. Why? Might it be that she is the epitome of the woman who lives on the fringe of other people's lives, helping to shape their destiny, but no more than that?

Polonius in
Hamlet

TONY CHURCH

TONY CHURCH, now an Associate Artist, was a founder member of the Royal Shakespeare Company in 1960. He brought to the Company experience gained in both modern and Shakespearean plays; and over the years he has recorded major roles in 26 of the complete plays of Shakespeare for Argo, appeared in a number of television productions, and worked as Director of the Northcott Theatre, Exeter. He is Director of the Guildhall School of Drama. At Stratford he has acted at both the Royal Shakespeare Theatre and The Other Place, and has played many of his roles in the Company's Newcastle and London seasons, as well as on tour at home and abroad. His wide range of work for the Royal Shakespeare Company includes the King in *Henry IV*, Sir Toby Belch, Antonio in *The Merchant of Venice*, Friar Laurence, Don Armado, Ulysses, and Gloucester, besides modern parts and the title role of *King Lear* at The Other Place. He has played Polonius in two Royal Shakespeare Theatre productions of *Hamlet*. The first, in 1965, was directed by Peter Hall with David Warner as Hamlet and John Bury as designer; the second, with Michael Pennington as Hamlet and Ralph Koltai as designer, was directed by John Barton in 1980.

I have been extraordinarily lucky to have had the chance to play Polonius three times already, at the ages of fifteen at school, thirty-five at Stratford-upon-Avon and the Aldwych, and again at both places at fifty. I say 'already' advisedly – another chance at sixty-five or seventy would not come amiss!

Under the influence of an enlightened headmaster I had been taught, in 1945, that Hamlet's view of the other characters in the play was suspect; therefore, when playing in the Hurstpierpoint College production in that same year, I offered a sympathetic view of the role, encouraged by A. J. Hill, my first director. The notice in the College magazine says, I now see,

103

18 'Marry, sir, here's my drift'
Tony Church as Polonius, August 1965

'Church used his peculiar voice to great advantage.' My memory is that I included the verbal mannerisms of one of my teachers – maybe the one who wrote the notice! Studying Tudor and Stuart history later for my Higher Certificate, I came to the conclusion that there was famous precedent for my imitations – that Shakespeare had intended a portrait, at least in part, of Lord Burghley, the best-known statesman of his time.

The arguments for Polonius as Burghley have been well rehearsed (and accorded the accolade of Dover Wilson's edition) – and well attacked by Keith Brown (in *English Studies* 55 of 1974): he favours the Polish-born Danish diplomat Henrik Ramel as Shakespeare's source. The possibility that William Kemp, a likely candidate for casting as Polonius, may have met Ramel in Denmark is a fascinating 'tease'. Brown may be on to a more likely explanation, but in *character*, and as a fertilizer for the actor's imagination, Burghley's story is too rich to ignore. He was an official under the very Protestant regime of Edward VI; although disbarred under Catholic Mary he was respected, and even consulted occasionally; he rapidly became the principal adviser to Queen Elizabeth. She referred to him as the Fox ('hide fox and all after!'), and other courtiers called him Pondus or Ponderosus; he sent a servant called Windebank to spy on his son in Paris; his burial at Stamford, according to some authorities, coincided with his funeral at Westminster Abbey – so where was the real body? A 'hugger-mugger' affair if you like. He even offered a series of 'precepts' to his son which seem to parallel the advice to Laertes in spirit even more than in letter:

Precept V: Be sure you keep some great man always to your friend, yet trouble him not for trifles; compliment him often, present him with many, yet small, gifts, and of little charge, and if you have cause to bestow any great gratuity on him then let it be no chest commodity or obscure thing, but such a one as may be daily in sight, the better to be remembered . . .
Precept VI: Neither undertake law against any man before you be fully resolved you have the right on your side, which being once so ascertained, then spare neither cost nor pains to accomplish it.
Precept VII: Beware of suretyship for your best friend . . .
Precept VIII: Towards your superiors be humble yet generous; with your equals familiar yet respective; towards your inferiors show much humility, with some familiarity . . .
Precept X: Be not scurrilous in conversation, nor satirical in your wits . . . jests when they do savour of too much truth leave a bitterness in the minds of those that are touched.

Many of Burghley's state papers are incredibly convoluted and Polonial; the working and reworking of the warrant for the execution of Mary Queen of Scots show what can happen to language under the twin stresses of danger and political manoeuvre.

I found this wondrously useful in the famous 'letter scene': Burghley was terrified of the Queen's reaction; Polonius was desperately trying to recover lost ground – the effect is similar. The complexities of this scene (2.2.85–167) are often just silly in performance. Silliness, to read theatrical criticism, would seem to be the playing-inheritance of the role – every time an actor redeems Polonius from this charge he is applauded, or criticized, as if the effect were new. Yet if Polonius *is* a fool, what does that make Claudius, who employs him and obviously relies on his judgement, or the Queen, who refers to him as a 'good old man' and trusts him in her bedchamber? Eric Shorter, in an article in the *Daily Telegraph* in August 1980 ('Getting to the heart of Polonius') says 'In recent years the character has come to be recognized more and more as an important political figure', but is this recognition so recent? I believe there have always been actors who have known the measure of the man – more often than critics. I remember Felix Aylmer more as an old fox than an old fool in Olivier's 1948 film; Alan Webb was a very serious statesman in Alec Guinness's production of 1951; André van Gyseghem was affectionate *and* politic in Buzz Goodbody's 1975 production at The Other Place. In the nineteenth century, actors J. H. Barnes and Joseph Munden both decided that Polonius's apparent stupidities were a mask to hide his real thoughts and to flatter the intelligence of his hearers.

Apparent stupidities? Does Polonius then *know* that he is being funny, and trade on the effect? In Peter Hall's production of 1965–6, with David Warner as Hamlet, this was definitely the idea. In our initial discussions, Peter made it clear that, for him, the Establishment against which Hamlet ranged himself was well nigh impregnable, and that Polonius was its epitome. We talked of the thirteen years of bland Conservative government that had recently ceased, the image of which was Harold Macmillan, taking fellow statesmen and friends to see *Beyond the Fringe*, and laughing very loudly at the impersonation of himself. The languid upper-class accent, the drooping eyelids, the fondness for the grouse-moors, concealed the sharpest political intelligence of his day; but in the end he overreached himself in the attempt to control his succession as party leader. 'A dangerous old smoothie', said the director, 'Polonius is a natural enemy to Hamlet. Basically a knave and a manipulator, he may even be an opportunist, suggesting, in a roundabout and falsely-modest way, his daughter as a marriage prospect for Hamlet, by the very process of forbidding her to be his mistress; certainly the Queen appears to approve of the affair in his presence.' (Burghley, incidentally, was well known for manoeuvring his daughter Anne about the court at one stage.)

These Machiavellian considerations in 1965 did not help Polonius to be as funny as we had hoped, until late in the rehearsal process (a strong vein of comedy in the first two hours and more of the play is surely Shakespeare's intention – and sorely needed). A strange but simple decision helped to achieve what we wanted – the drinks were changed. Now the incessant toping of the Danish court was not only well known to Hamlet – every Elizabethan knew of it, and of Christian IV's insistence on salvoes of artillery to accompany the bouts. What we had been using in rehearsal were goblets of (supposed) wine (following the text 'he drains his draughts of Rhenish down'), but one morning we found glass decanters and small spirit glasses on side tables in every scene. 'From now on', said our director, 'everyone drinks schnapps (aquavit) – and very quickly.' I think, in one day, I doubled my speaking-rate: Polonius started to speak with the panache and lightning intricacy of the best, albeit most eccentric, of university lecturers. He compressed his lengthy verbal manoeuvrings into the same time as other people took to be simple. The reactions to him of King, Queen, and Hamlet speeded up as a result, points were scored lightly and efficiently, and the laughter started.

The other special feature of the 1965 interpretation did not emerge until the first night. Instead of simply wishing me good luck Peter Hall said, at the door of my dressing-room, 'I want you tonight to consider one element more than any other – he's been behind the arras *before*.' I knew, on a moment's reflection, that he did not mean the arras in the lobby – what he meant was that sexual curiosity was the driving force. Now the Polonius of this production was an oppressive Victorian-style paterfamilias, who held his daughter on a tight rein and lectured his son: but the underbelly of Victorian life was sexually vicious, and the comparison seemed to hold. The heavy, moralizing father wanted the *details* of Hamlet's behaviour to Ophelia, and of Laertes' escapades in the brothels of Paris. I can affirm that sexual prurience was a wonderful source of energy – and more lasting than schnapps.

The *appearance* of Polonius fitted neatly into the overall design of this production. The set was black and shiny, covered with formica; all the doors fitted flush, there were no ledges or edges, nothing to grasp, nowhere to gain a foothold; Polonius was dressed in an underrobe of official pinstripe trouser material, with an overrobe edged with maroon and silver;

his beard was black and silver, his eyebrows silver and drooping, his official cap fitted close to his head showing no trace of errant locks; Claudius's fair hair was equally plastered down, the Queen's in as tight a style, Ophelia's formal and set. Polonius looked as if insults would slide off him, and in the scenes with Hamlet they did. After the exchange 'What do you read, my lord?', 'Words, words, words', Polonius asks, 'What is the matter, my lord?'; Hamlet, deliberately misunderstanding, replies 'Between whom?' 'I mean the matter that you read, my lord', says Polonius, laughing as if to say, 'I know you are mocking me', so the noise of the laughter was weary and patronizing. After the reference to the 'Crab' going 'backward', Polonius's aside, 'Though this be madness, yet there's method in't', meant 'He cannot fool me.' The watchword was, as Humpty Dumpty said, 'Impenetrability'. Certain details reinforced his position as a respected statesman. Reynaldo was formal and discreet, dressed in sub- dued imitation of his master; there were often other councillors present to back up Polonius in court, in particular in the flurry of decisions after the disturbance of the play scene; most noticeable was the intense concentra- tion with which Claudius listened to his every word. After his death, Osric appeared similarly dressed, in respect for the tradition; the world of Polonius survived. Here the director took his cue from Martin Holmes (*The Guns of Elsinore*) in his insistence on the fact that, even after Laertes' revelations, when Hamlet wounds Claudius, the court *all* cry 'Treason! Treason!'

When I was offered the opportunity to play the part again fifteen years later, I was extremely apprehensive. The whole experience of 1965 had been unforgettable and, unusually, so had the text (the actor's computer normally 'wipes the tape' when a play comes out of the repertoire and other work takes over). To my surprise, after a relatively short discussion with John Barton, the 1980 director, the whole picture looked different. Over- efficient government no longer seemed the threat it had been – Nixon had proved an inefficient Machiavel, Russia had lost its footing in Afghanistan, the Common Market was crumbling. Individual enthusiasms and failures, the collapse of best intentions, the breakdown of *happy* families seemed more important; Hamlet's agony appeared to be romantic and destructive, rather than politically rebellious.

Barton pointed to the *narrative* as the key: Polonius's death provoked madness in Ophelia, and in Laertes the leadership of a rebellion. Surely this must mean there had been great love in the children for their father? The eccentricities, the long-windedness, etc., of the man could be endearing, as well as showing the excesses of an official style; the concern for Ophelia's reputation could be as much an expression of parental care as the mercantile insurance of her virginity; the sending of Reynaldo to report on Laertes could be not so much prurience as an earthy, physical man's desire to know that his son is sowing his wild oats well. Finally, Barton said he wanted Hamlet to regret the death of Polonius, and the audience to regret it too.

To achieve this, a great deal of work went into the first domestic scene between Polonius, Laertes and Ophelia. Ophelia entered in a loose white dress, with long flowing fair hair, carrying a lute, followed by Laertes in travelling coat carrying a suitcase and a bag of foils. They were physically affectionate, and she teased him about practising what he preached. Polonius entered, whistling a happy tune (to be used later for 'Tomorrow is St Valentine's day'), took off his plum-coloured overrobe, and revealed a brown workaday suit, bedecked with watch chain and spectacles on a cord. He wore no hat, his hair was fuzzy and white, with white beard and quizzical eyebrows. In the advice to Laertes it was clear that Polonius knew his children were smiling behind his back, and that he did not mind. During the words 'Beware of entrance to a quarrel', etc., he drew a rapier from Laertes' bag and delivered a fake thrust at the boy, who then pretended that he had been wounded or even killed: he pulled his overcoat over his head and pretended to fall off his suitcase on which he was sitting. The laughter shared by father and children was always shared by the audience as well. At the end of the advice, Polonius says:

> This above all: to thine own self be true,
> And it must follow, as the night the day,
> Thou canst not then be false to any man. (1.3.78–80)

In the 1965 production I had delivered those lines as a direct appeal to naked self-interest; in 1980 I spoke them as a simple moral truth which I knew my son would share with me. After Laertes' departure there followed a little sequence much commented on by observers: Ophelia took up the lute once more and hummed the tune later to be heard in the mad scene ('How should I your true love know?'). Polonius, working away at some state papers, whistled in unison with her, the world stood still for a moment, and father and daughter were in harmony. Polonius then asked the damaging question: 'What is't, Ophelia, he hath said to you?' Frequently, this was greeted with laughter – the sly old man was not so relaxed as he seemed, and Ophelia was not to escape without an explanation; this, we thought, produced the right balance between affection and interest. As the inquisition progressed, Polonius's attitude was to assume that she must be worldly enough to understand that princes are not to be trusted:

> These blazes, daughter,
> Giving more light than heat, extinct in both . . .
> You must not take for fire   (1.3.117–18, 120)

was delivered to the accompaniment of a playful rubbing of noses. At his next line –

> For Lord Hamlet,
> Believe so much in him, that he is young,
> And with a larger tether may he walk
> Than may be given you –   (1.3.123–6)

Ophelia turned away in embarrassed silence, and Polonius issued the instruction: 'This is for all: I would not, in plain terms . . . have you . . . give words or talk with the Lord Hamlet' – and in tones of high temper. We had offered a portrait of a loving and humorous father who nevertheless was to be obeyed without question.

The sense of fun soon came back in the Reynaldo scene, where the predominant note was of a father enjoying his son's peccadilloes. Even when the old man forgot his lines, the affection that existed between master and servant was not destroyed. Once more, in a brief moment between Reynaldo's departure and Ophelia's arrival, Polonius whistled to himself as he picked up his robe. The appalling news that Hamlet has apparently been driven mad by Ophelia's rejection leads Polonius in the *text* straight into the problem of reporting this event to the King; here we added the business of the father covering his poor frightened daughter with his robes of state, and leading her protectively from the stage. Later, in the mad scene, Ophelia appeared wearing her dead father's robe, and it was only after the first night that I remembered that Glenda Jackson, the Ophelia in 1965, had used the same business. This led me to reflect on the nature of parental oppression; Glenda's reasoning was based on the suffocation of her spirit by her father – that although he had frightened her, she could not escape him. My Polonius of 1980, it could be said, overpowered his daughter in the end by too much love.

It has been argued that the 1980 Polonius would not have set up his daughter so callously as a decoy for Hamlet in the nunnery scene. My answer to this is that in the conflict of loyalties Polonius's professional duty

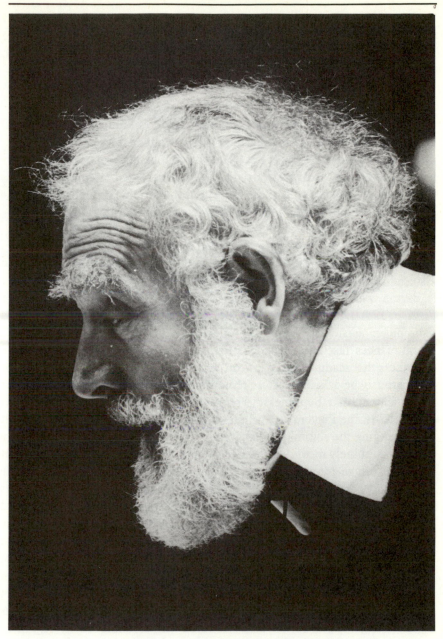

19   'How now, Ophelia, what's the matter?'
Tony Church as Polonius, June 1980

to the *state* emerges victorious. He has made a mistake, with the best of intentions, in ordering his daughter to reject Hamlet's advances: it can, however, provide an explanation of Hamlet's madness that will be a relief to everybody. The Queen hopes Polonius's explanation is right; but the King must be convinced. A much more awkward problem for a loving father comes later: why, when Hamlet rushes from the stage having brutally abused Ophelia, does Polonius wait for a soliloquy by Ophelia before going to comfort his daughter? Why even then does he address only one and a half lines directly to her ('How now Ophelia? You need not tell us what Lord Hamlet said, we heard it all')? I compensated by comforting her physically, while speaking to the King; but the problem remains, particularly as Hamlet not only berated Ophelia in this production but slapped her face very hard as well. I put it down, in the end, to the effect of the King's anger. I also let my own anger rise, until it was more immediate than my daughter's suffering. This provided the fuel for the succeeding scenes, and also radically altered my relationship with Hamlet.

Barton was very concerned that the Polonius/Hamlet story should *develop*, rather than start as opposition, as it had done in 1965. In the fishmonger scene I regarded Hamlet as a mad lover, and found his extravagances fascinating ('how pregnant sometimes his replies are! A happiness that madness often hits on, which reason and sanity could not so prosperously be delivered of'). I remember Barton saying to me, 'Polonius rather envies that happiness.' Hamlet treated Polonius as an amiable eccentric. In the Players' arrival scene, I wore their fool's cap and bauble whilst singing the actors' praises, joined in a 'cross-talk' act with Hamlet, and was genuinely moved at the First Player's breakdown. All this was in great contrast to 1965, where the line, 'Look where he has not turned his colour, and has tears in his eyes', was delivered with philistine distaste.

From the end of the nunnery scene, however, the Poloniuses of 1965 and 1980 came together – in hatred of Hamlet and determination to see him deported, or imprisoned at least. In fact, the anger of a loving father, added to the previous force of political necessity, proved a formidable combination. When Polonius entered, after the play, into the scene between Rosencrantz, Guildenstern and Hamlet, and was met with word-play superficially like that of the fishmonger scene, he rejected it totally: to Hamlet's final 'or like a whale?' he answered with crushing scorn, '*very* like a whale'. Polonius, in my judgement, by this time had had enough.

There are many contradictions in the role: a loving, but overbearing father; a practical, but long-winded and egotistical politician; a university actor, whose production of the nunnery scene goes very wrong; a philosophical observer, but also a voyeur; a manipulator, and yet strangely an innocent; an old expert, and 'a great baby'. Of course they are just the contradictions that make up a fully-realized character. Critics and performers have all worried at these contradictions over the years. Because it conflicted with the 'foolish' interpretation, the advice to Laertes was often cut in late-eighteenth and nineteenth-century productions. Polonius's behaviour is described by Dr Johnson as 'Not folly, but dotage encroaching on wisdom'; by Coleridge as 'the personified memory of wisdom no longer possessed'. Thomas Davies described the eighteenth-century actor James Taswell in the role as 'A fool with a dash of the knave'. My favourite, however, is Macklin, whose impression was of 'Oddity grafted on the man of sense'.

The reaction of theatre critics to the 1965 performance was in the main appreciative of its intentions, though often in disagreement with them: 'Why should Hamlet tease such a consummate string-puller, when the insults slide off his well-oiled back?' (Alan Brien, *Sunday Telegraph*); 'It ran counter to all the lines' (Milton Shulman, *Evening Standard*); 'A tough court official, quite different from the one Shakespeare intended' (B. A. Young, *Financial Times*). We are once more in the territory of reading the parts according to Hamlet's description of them. Yet even then there was extraordinary variation: 'A grand comedy part' (*Nottingham Evening Post*), 'An extraordinarily sympathetic Polonius' (*Oxford Mail*) – *not* my intention! – 'A wrily foolish Polonius' (*Yorkshire Post*), 'Almost as big a bore to the audience as he is to the court' (*Oxford Times*). To me the most perceptive (i.e. he saw my intention!) was John Higgins in the *Financial Times* in 1966: 'Everyone apart from Hamlet is putting on an act. Polonius may bumble and chuckle at his own jokes, but this is simply a disguise chosen by a master intriguer.' The 1980 performance was less lengthily described, but better liked: 'Almost the only figure with whom you can feel a sustained sympathy' (Eric Shorter, *Daily Telegraph*); 'Pragmatic, firm and stern' (*Yorkshire Post*); 'A poignant father/daughter relationship that I have never before seen depicted' (Gareth Lloyd-Evans, *Stratford-upon-Avon Herald*); 'Affectionate, courteous, and even wise' (B. A. Young, *Financial Times*); 'More loving father than meddling old fool, and as great a lover of actors as the Prince' (Irving Wardle, *The Times*); and even 'Much more Hamlet's philosophical equal than Horatio' (Mel Gussow, *New York Sunday Times*)!

My reaction to the part is conditioned not only by playing Polonius three times, but by the good fortune I have had to combine the role within the last four years with those of Gloucester in *King Lear* and York in *Richard II*. I believe Shakespeare to have had a special fondness for chief ministers, in particular those whose family relationships impinged on the affairs of state. Gloucester's failure to understand his legitimate son, and his over-fondness for the product of his lust, combines with his loyalty to the King to result in his blinding; York, caught between his loyalty to Richard and his belief that Bolingbroke has been wronged, sides with Bolingbroke and is then compelled to inform on his son's treachery to the new regime; Polonius sacrifices his daughter's happiness to political necessity, and is killed whilst trying to prove his theories correct. Each one of these deeply political creatures suffers through honest service and a conflict of the best of intentions. In an age when politicians are universally regarded with contempt, it is refreshing to find that once there was a true genius to whom no human activity was beyond compassion. Shakespeare loved his men of affairs, and perhaps of all of them Polonius was his favourite. I can certainly vouch, after thirty-six years' acquaintance with the role, that it is one of the most rewarding of all parts to play.

POSTSCRIPT I have been asked by many people what the actor playing Polonius does with his time between his death and the end of the play. In the old touring days, and probably in Shakespeare's highly economical company, he frequently reappeared as the Gravedigger – the comedian's 'double'. I occupied much of *my* time searching the text for those 'concealed characters' typified by the list of the Danish army: Martial Stalk, General Censure, Sergeant Death, Corporal Agent, Private Swee ('Faith, her privates we'), Engineer Hoist ('with his own petard') and Cannoneer Without. The ladies of the court soon became equally visible: Felicity Awhile, Virgin Crantz (sister to Rosencrantz?), and Maiden Strewments, to name but a few. A complete list awaits a publisher and detailed scholastic appraisal.

Hamlet

MICHAEL PENNINGTON

ICHAEL PENNINGTON made his first appearance in a Royal Shakespeare Company production of *Hamlet* as Fortinbras, in 1965. He had joined the Company in the previous year; but it was not until 1974 that he began to develop his career within it, gaining experience not only in both the Stratford theatres but also in Newcastle, at the Aldwych and at the Warehouse. He has also reached a wide audience through his television appearances, his readings, his one-man show (*Diary of a Madman*) and his book, *Rossya – A Journey Through Siberia*, published in 1977. His work for the Royal Shakespeare Company covers plays of all periods, in which he has played a variety of roles. His principal Shakespearean parts include Angelo in 1974, Mercutio in 1976, Berowne in 1978, and, in the same season, the Duke in *Measure for Measure*. His Hamlet followed in 1980. The production, designed by Ralph Koltai and with a cast including Derek Godfrey as Claudius, Barbara Leigh-Hunt as Gertrude, Carol Royle as Ophelia and Tony Church as Polonius, was directed by John Barton.

Hamlet is a white-magic play, as white as *Macbeth* is black. *Macbeth* remains an unholy riddle that we still hesitate to name for fear of retribution; but *Hamlet* is potently on the side of life, for all its catastrophes, and clearly occupies a special place in the lives of those who have to do with it. Among actors, the central part is supposedly the object of much professional rivalry; among those who have played it, it is the source, surprisingly often, of regret, and occasionally of real self-definition. Directors seem to identify with the play and the character as much as actors; most productions have their directors' sensibilities written all over them, and everyone is agreed the play should show the age and body of the time his form and pressure as well as, inevitably, refracting the personal preoccupations of those working on it. From an habituated audience it still

20   'What's Hecuba to him, or he to Hecuba?'
Michael Pennington as Hamlet, June 1980

calls out a nervy sense of expectation; and, perhaps more important, to a young audience it can give a theatrical taste that will last a lifetime.

Occasionally an actor may come to the part innocently, having neither seen it nor played anything in it before; but this must be exceptional, and an accumulated peripheral knowledge of the play is a burden most Hamlets arrive with. I had had a shot at it at twenty, as a student, and I suppose in hindsight this was the beginning of a preparation. However, perhaps mercifully, I can remember little about that occasion except a sense of surprise when I found that the playing of the part was enjoyable, fun, a release; at that stage I in no way associated acting with enjoyment, more with the direst self-analysis, and I was astonished not to feel more of a failure. I couldn't believe it. Now I can, because I can see that the part had in some sense contracted to fit the lineaments of a twenty-year-old, just as it has a way of expanding or tightening to suit the extraordinary variety of bodies that have climbed into it. In that limited sense the character is extremely obliging – the greatest straight role ever written – which does not contradict the fact that finally to pull it off will take the actor further down into his psyche, memory and imagination, and further outwards to the limits of his technical knowledge and equipment, than he has probably been before.

A couple of other involvements with the play in the interim being really neither here nor there, I came to the part again inside a company with which I had been absorbed for five years, with a director with whom I already had a working relationship, and with the part in a sense having been quietly bubbling away since my student days. The readiness was, it was to be hoped, all. So that by the time John Barton and I began a series of roughly weekly meetings in the January before April rehearsals, a certain amount of preparation could be said to have been done, in a way that could not be said of other projects. Many of these meetings were, on the face of it, surprisingly inconclusive. I recalled that, in the case of Barry Kyle's *Measure for Measure* two years previously, a number of firm decisions, clarifying images, had formed between us before rehearsals began, in response to the riddles of the play and the elusive character of the Duke; but this tentative shaping up to Hamlet, although based on a good working knowledge of the play, produced mostly caveats, a few long-range hunches, and naturally a determination to open the book freshly and forget the past. The closer we moved at this time to definitions of character and ambience, the more my imagination contracted and the play seemed to burst out of our confining thoughts. As we veered away from these issues, the cutting of the text became a priority. An early impulse of mine to play the uncut text having been rightly dismissed as a Wagnerian folly, it was soon agreed that there was a need to cut radically, preferably by means of filleting rather than major surgery, and pretty soon John Barton had come up with a text from which hardly more than half a dozen lines at a stretch had gone, but which would have a Stratford audience on the street by eleven o'clock without any cherished area of the play having been brutalized. (Amidst these rigours there were some whimsical moments. A passage from the bad quarto in the advice to the Players about their jester 'blabbering with his lips, and thus keeping in his cinquepace of jests' was deemed so baroque and unfamiliar that it was left in – until after a month of rehearsal it was decided it was a great nuisance and should be dumped.)

Some specific ideas were floated at this time which have survived: the Ghost was to be as alarmingly human as possible and should be seen by Gertrude as by everyone else; the Players are professionals and should be good at their job, even though they have lost their base and are on the road; and there seemed no reason to suppose that Hamlet himself does not have the predominantly graceful qualities in his make-up credited to him by Ophelia, Horatio and Fortinbras. Generally speaking, though, it seemed the best service we could do ourselves was to lay off and let the play operate on us, through us, in rehearsal. In line with this, the setting would probably need to be simple, very simple; and in the obvious absence of theoretical overlay, the narrative would be likely to be clear and swift, catching its audience by surprise, however well they knew the story.

We finally edged sidelong into rehearsal by means of small meetings of two or three characters at a time – Hamlet and Ophelia, Gertrude and Claudius, Hamlet and Rosencrantz and Guildenstern – rather than with a read-through or head-on company call; and a rather unassuming enquiry into the connections between us and into the groundplan of the play was, I suppose, the feature of the early days. In the face of the play's riches, we needed to be fairly hard-nosed. Every famous passage and every operatic opportunity for the actor was to be tested against its contribution to the story or to the development of a relationship, and the relationships themselves were to be explored in tight harness to the action. I had to trick myself into being as naïve as possible; to grasp simply the A to B of every passage; to try to identify the precise *purpose* of, say, the closet scene, and so free myself from its famousness in the hope of approaching Hamlet's alienation, his struggle with himself and the others, and his particular bravery, only through what lay in front of me on the page. Grace-notes could wait.

Inevitably, we found that Shakespeare had been there before us; each famous passage does of course contain its particular momentum, its own means of pressing the events forward. The play began forming itself in my mind as a brilliant narrative exploding on the one hand into set pieces like the first court scene, the play scene and the duel; and sustained on the other by a series of essential interviews, duologues that define Hamlet's relations with his neighbours – the Ghost, Ophelia and Gertrude above all, but also Polonius, Rosencrantz and Guildenstern, Horatio and the Gravediggers: a kind of character dialectic that is further refined at four crucial moments into Hamlet's purest and most distinctive encounters, those with his audience. These form the character's most confidential relationship; and in practice it meant preparing to meet the audience on terms as open and mutual as possible. Given what we know of the social circumstances of Shakespeare's theatre, and given the immediacy that a theatrical event should have at any time, it still seems natural to expect at least half an answer to his blazing questions:

> Am I a coward?
> Who calls me villain? Breaks my pate across? . . .
> Tweaks me by the nose? Gives me the lie i' the throat
> As deep as to the lungs? Who does me this?
> Ha? (2.2.571–6)

Once this had begun to emerge, specific questions of design became clearer. The physical setting needed to be open enough to accommodate the sweep of the set pieces, uncluttered enough to focus sharply on the interviews (a bed would be an unwanted third character in the closet scene) and confrontational enough to allow as close a contact as possible with the house for the soliloquies. The costumes would tend to reflect character and humour rather than a social or political moment. Very soon a raked platform in front of a large open space was modelled.

Meanwhile, moving through rehearsals, John Barton was becoming more and more interested in the theatre image that was to become central to the production – the sense in which the chance arrival of a troupe of players at the court not only provokes action in the dramatic narrative sense, a means to catch the conscience of the King, but also precipitates in Hamlet an enquiry into the validity of his own emotions next to the supposedly counterfeit ones of the actors, into his own role as avenger, and into the

21 'My lord, I have news to tell you'
Hamlet with Polonius (Tony Church)

appearance of his world as against its corrupt reality. At the time I did not really understand this theme and rather feared it, thinking it might draw us into a sort of Pirandellian 'angle' on the play, and not really seeing how it helped; but it became very important to me later. Among other things, it gives a clue to the peculiar balances in some of Hamlet's language; though he is rarely highly poetic in the manner of Lear or Macbeth, there are vertiginous switches in him from the humdrum to the hypermetaphorical and back which I could understand better when I saw that he sees himself simultaneously as a private man and also as a miscast avenging angel in some atavistic tragedy:

> Now could I drink hot blood,
> And do such bitter business as the day
> Would quake to look on. Soft! Now to my mother . . .   (3.2.390–2)

Often too his sharp perception of the immediate physical world is linked to a literary taste:

> or e'er those shoes were old
> With which she followed my poor father's body,
> Like Niobe, all tears . . .   (1.2.147–9)

Clearly the distinction between self-dramatization and real feeling, theatricality and life, runs right through the play, and was beginning to influence my reception of the text; and soon the theatrical world itself – hampers, cloaks and property swords – began to appear in rehearsals.

This initial hesitation in picking up an idea of the director's may serve to illustrate the working relationship of actor and director a little. Without a base of agreement in most matters a venture such as this would be fraught with all sorts of danger – inadvisable in fact; and the fact in this case of having worked with John Barton before, and having discussed things at length before rehearsal, was, mutually I hope, reassuring. But differences there will always be, if only of bias – a conflict one hopes will be creative and without animus, either resolved by compromise or perhaps remaining through the production as a sort of mutual check and balance. Throughout rehearsals of the earlier part of the play John Barton would be inviting me wherever possible to take gentler options with the part, feeling for instance that I should find restraint and courtesy in the first court scene, albeit under great strain, while I was inclined towards sarcasm and sharpness. There may be no final resolution to this sort of thing – individual performances in a run will veer to and fro, and our debate continues. What was constant in John Barton's guidance of me was his encouragement always to use the language as a *necessary* funnel for the emotions in a scene. This may sound obvious, but in a part as emotionally turbulent as Hamlet the actor may sometimes allow a tide of feeling to distort highly-wrought areas of language and so make them obscure. In fact of course the feelings *require* those words, and only those words, to define them and make them communicable – it is all one thing, the feeling, the pressure, the need to speak, the image that defines. It can be like pressing a tornado through the eye of a needle, but a persistent attention to colour, texture, rhythm and characteristic music goes beyond textual piety to become an emotional necessity.

Other things were emerging. Characterization is difficult to talk about in relation to Hamlet, for the player is working in a specially subjective way, and the production is likely to be reflecting his own basic personality. It would be surprising to find him reaching very far from his theatrical self or a director asking him to do so. A man's Hamlet tends to be one of a kind, and the main challenge is to express fully the deep crises of the part through your own spirit. Nevertheless, there is a responsibility too, and periods of objectivity. The essentially *young* man of the opening seemed to me the least like the prime mover of a tragedy. Grief seems to have sharpened his sense of falsehood in the world around him, but in other ways the immeasurable shock he has received has sent him to sleep. The torpor is deep and disturbing to watch, lifting in utterances – 'My father, methinks I see my father' – which are more hallucinatory than sentimental. Anybody familiar with bereavement can recognize the symptoms. In dramatic terms, until the news of the Ghost's appearance animates him, gives him something to believe in, he is a dramatic hero of whom nothing much can be expected. During the early stages of the play the pressure of events makes him into a hero of whom much *must* be expected, and yet his characteristic response to challenge is to step back, into 'wild and whirling words', secretiveness, and indeed to fall in all too easily with a series of chance encounters in Act 2, Scene 2 which allows him almost to forget himself – until right at the end of the 'rogue and peasant slave' soliloquy a glimmer of purpose appears. This moment seemed to us to demand the first of two theatre intervals, leaving an image on the eye of a still man in the act of beginning to walk.

So the man of the first third of the play is non-initiating, relatively passive, immobilized by his burdens; and if he is a rebel, whether the production is politically inclined or not, he is a very conservative rebel. He has a yearning for the past that seems to go beyond his personal crisis to be a cultural need. His world is based not only on a contemporary sense of reason but also on an older, deeper morality, and his vision is traduced by a new world of sexually aggressive men, court espionage and seemingly opportunistic women. A deep concern for the past and its values runs through him and he perhaps never speaks of the future. As a physical consequence of this idea, we began to get a picture of a man in the first court scene who was soberly and traditionally dressed amid the tawdry theatricality of the new court; and in general an almost formal courtesy and restraint began to creep into my dealings with acquaintances and visitors to the court, alongside an open enthusiasm for my friends. Hamlet has a kind of sweet optimism, bitterly disappointed; and the struggle to *overcome* the maelstrom inside him seems truer, and potentially more moving, than a continual public display of his demons.

On the other hand, it became obvious in rehearsing the scenes with Ophelia and Gertrude that alongside the evident generosity and grace in the man there was now a strong current of violence, particularly towards the women in his life, aggravated by a sense of betrayal, and sadly misdirected towards them rather than towards his real enemy. In the nunnery scene we moved towards an openly expressed viciousness – the tenderness of the early part of the scene turned on its head – and it occurred to me that this is paralleled in the still more violent language of the closet, where the arrival of the Ghost perhaps forestalls another physical outbreak. It seemed a rich streak for the production to mine, not least because the opportunity for the audience to question the hero's morality, and even to project an antipathy back to the stage, is an important counterpoint to the mainly sympathetic appeal on which the part rests. Conversely again, his generosity in unbetrayed friendship, as with Horatio, remains to me one of the most touching things about Hamlet; he protects his less imaginative friend from his 'curious considerations', the darker recesses of his thinking, so that, even on the edge of catastrophe at the end of the play, he will not let Horatio take the strain of his premonitions – 'Let be'. It is a spirit both highly demanding and very solicitous, its artistic potential cruelly wasted.

All these things were developing out of a daily exposure to the play in as innocent a frame of mind as possible, and all the time hints were being thrown out that sent us ferreting through the play for corroboration. What was the man's characteristic language? While John Barton was pointing out to me how often theatrical words were recurring in the script – 'cue', 'act', 'action' – I too was out hunting, finding how often Hamlet returns to 'dust', to 'nothing', to triplets – 'well, well, well', 'except my life, except my life, except my life', and noting that in three of the four confessional soliloquies – but never elsewhere – he emphatically uses the word 'coward'. Then again, what is one to make of the sudden explosion of three lines of ferocious monosyllables in 'How all occasions do inform against me':

> I do not know
> Why yet I live to say 'This thing's to do',
> Sith I have cause and will and strength and means
> To do't . . .   (4.4.43–6)

These are small bricks in a big wall, but necessary; and I suppose at this time we were going in some sort of sequence from early hunches to a radar scanning of the text to a grasp of the converging lines of the part.

It all sounds fairly calculated, this daytime enquiry; my night-time exposure to the play was rather different. Waiting for the emotional flashpoints that would bring all these things together, I found myself writing Hamlet-riddles in an attempt to rein the kaleidoscopic impressions of the day into some sort of documentary coherence:

The external world is proceeding smoothly. The society is attractive, warmhearted, congenial; they all understand one another. The really difficult thing is to stand apart from such a seductive world. Nevertheless one man, already grief-stricken and prey to morbid reflection, has a nightmare in which he receives a message, supposedly from beyond the grave, which declares that the external world is in fact riddled with corruption, its leader a murderer and adulterer, and his wife guilty by implication. It is inconceivable. Vainly the benighted dreamer scans the external world for corroboration of his fantastic dream but finds none. The external world is the same as it was before. Nobody acknowledges even the possibility of guilt. Even a carefully prepared entertainment devised to expose the guilty is taken simply as a piece of social bad taste. The man must be mistaken, and his dream truly a nightmare. He persuades himself otherwise, his reason totters and he begins to despair. Events overtake him and he finds himself caught up in an adventure story that finally destroys him. Before dying he does in fact destroy his enemy, though still without having any conclusive proof of that man's original guilt or the woman's involvement. By the time he dies the man has killed three people and indirectly caused the death of others. He still has not exposed the original crime to the eyes of the world. He has only trusted his instinct, in the form of a visitation from the other world that is most akin to a dream, and by an extraordinary and deep irony, his instinct was true.

Could we really be meaning to confront critics and audiences with yet another *Hamlet* without an angle beyond our developing hunches? Should we not have a couple of tricks up our sleeves? The play is swamped in a miasma of interpretation – this director's line, this actor's forte, 350 years of all kinds of enquiry. *Hamlet* as a good yarn? How plain can plain theatre get? But then how good it would be if we could ambush our audiences into catching their breath at a turn in the story that their conscious minds have known since school, but which under theatrical pressure they have forgotten. And there is always a new, younger, audience too. Anyway, what was I myself on the verge of, asking all these questions? I was beginning to taste the famous isolation of the part, feeling the emotional tides of a man adrift from the behaviour, the humour, the very language of his neighbours: a disorientation that in some equivalent way was beginning to separate me from colleagues and friends:

Nothing could have less to do with ghosts, shadows, uncertainty of mind, the jolting of the earth beneath your feet, doubt between dream and waking, than the bright busy practicality of this court, with its clear vocabulary and shared purposes. The family is intact – Claudius with my mother, Polonius with Laertes and Ophelia – good humour and self-confidence everywhere. In this easy and comfortable world, a man dressed stubbornly in black, white with tiredness and a grinding grief, speaks in riddles: worms, skulls, words of leaping, boggling insanity uttered in tones of even normality. He is like a damaged animal they would leave for dead rather than take a step to save – a madman at a chamber concert.

But then dawn would break and each day we would have another go. By this time, a couple of weeks before previews, frequent run-throughs were planned, largely to allow me to have a look at the course. The formidable athletic geometry of the part requires a training to match, and I needed to know where the stress points lay, where the tricky corners were and where I could take a breath. The first third of the play is deceptive; as the character is passive, the central actor loses his usual responsibility for driving the play forward, and instead should be carried by it. But I soon found that the great middle arc of the play, from the nunnery through to the departure for England, was the most taxing stretch, the action moving precipitately in rhythm with Hamlet's direct organization of events. For the character, this progress is like a tunnel in which success lies next to defeat; where more violent impulses to action are checked by still deeper introspections; where the supernatural once again regulates the real world; where emotional and rational certainties are rocked once more. A rapprochement is unexpectedly reached with Gertrude which will alter the course of both their lives; and above all a murder is committed by accident which finally puts Hamlet outside his own moral framework for good and all. For the actor, this is where the part shakes you like a rat, racing you from one crisis to the next with scarcely time to draw breath; and at the end of the sequence both actor and character are washed up on the chilly plateau of 'How all occasions do inform against me', where rationality begins to seep back into the character and the actor once again meets the audience and is offered the prospect of rest. On the return from England, an eerie calm descends; but even here the earth is moving under his feet and violent action waits in ambush. Thinking forward as usual – narrative momentum always! – the actor has to realize that the point of the graveyard scene is not primarily Yorick, who is really a cadenza, but the discovery that the grave of 'one that was a woman' will turn out by a wicked irony to be ready for Ophelia, and that the fight in the grave, soon to be followed by the duel, is waiting just when he thought that things were settling down. It's not a part to play on an empty stomach.

In discussing the athletics rather than the aesthetics, I have moved out of rehearsal into describing the experience of performance, and indeed, these things being what they are, I remember little of the immediate run-up to opening except, as ever, the attempt to keep my performing head above water amidst the necessarily long hours and technical adjustments. The preview period is one of fourteen-hour days, re-rehearsal after the experience of meeting an audience, and changes to be absorbed before each evening; so that it is largely a matter of surviving. However, open we did, and at the time of writing I have played the part some 120 times and have not yet finished. Nevertheless, I will not really know much objectively about Hamlet until it is all over. Seen in retrospect for these purposes, the seemingly haphazard process of planning and rehearsal, with its chance discoveries, its missed opportunities, its dry calculations and intuitive hunches – a process that bemuses and frustrates outside observers, so invisible are its movements – might seem to have had some kind of form and pressure. However, a good deal of what I have described may never really have happened in rehearsal at all, but in performance – or been only realized in performance. Sustaining a role during a run is obviously the actor's province more particularly than the director's or critic's; and amidst all the interpreting and judgement, the actor is qualified by the experience of *Hamlet* for nothing except to go out the next day and do it again. He hopes that the peculiar gift bestowed on him is the aptitude to take a nightly jump in the dark, knowing only the broadest topography of the jump and little of the outcome. I do not know whether audiences realize, even in a relatively structured piece of work, the extent to which they, entering the building from one end, share with those entering from the other a real curiosity about the outcome of the evening. Certainly in playing the part I am more than usually aware of the narrowness of the margin separating a performance that is okay, even good, from one that is special – and how crucial the margin is, since no one wants to come so far to see a Hamlet that is just okay. People do expect to be changed, or at least moved over slightly. What the margin depends on goes beyond application and hard work into some speculative area too numinous to pursue. On some nights the part ups and plays you effortlessly; on others it is like labouring with an out-of-tune violin. Fortunately there is no knowing: on a night like the first, someone will come round and tell you you did nothing for them, and even in the latter case somebody may have been thrilled. An individual performance in the theatre is a live thing, with its own conditions and unpredictability; and to an extent the actor, given a base of discipline and control, must allow himself to be carried by the prevailing winds. Everyone wants the occasion to be special; everyone, including the actors, waits for lightning to strike.

At any event, a performance is one of a kind, and a slightly different man is presented every night; the emotional landscape the actor inhabits is variable, and this particularly volatile part has a way of changing shape in your hands. There are matters in the part that I have never in any case been happy to discuss, such as Hamlet's 'madness', which seems to me undiscussable outside the terms of performance. Whether Hamlet is 'mad', whatever that is, depends very much on how mad the spectator or actor happen to be. Sometimes it is the theatre's job to pass on a riddle, not to solve it. Certainly by the end of the cellarage scene Shakespeare has brought his character to a fork in the road – a man in extreme nervous disarray decides to feign a nervous breakdown. The irony is obvious. From there on, the exact contours of the divergence inside his personality are an option that as a performer I claim, just as I claim the right to vary within a discipline and over a period of time. The changes that take place through a run are not usually consciously planned, though in the repertoire system, with its frequent breaks, it is necessary to keep some kind of conscious stock; more frequently they arise, for better or worse, out of impulse – as on the evening when a sense of conscience suddenly replaced self-confidence in my attitude to the death of Rosencrantz and Guildenstern, and has remained ever since. The rationalization comes after. 'To be or not to be' varies quite a lot, possibly because it is really a relatively unimportant speech in the *line* of the part, though of course a beautiful thing in itself, and so it can afford to vary. Still, you do not notice a person ageing if you see them all the time, and a frequent attender of a production may be better placed than I am to assess changes in my performance. All that is really necessary for the actor working in repertoire is to be ready each time, to stay on his toes, in the knowledge that things will vary, and that the whole tissue of private references that underpin his performance will quietly change with the patterns of his own life and even the world news: 'What a piece of work is a man.' Above all he must retain a sense of occasion. There are many mistakes, many disappointments, a sense of defeat amidst the various elations. A particular kind of empathy between actor and audience seems to me crucial in this particular part, and therefore the actor's third ear, by which he monitors as far as he can the nature of the silence in the house on a particular night, the response to the comedy and so on – the strange process by which 1500 separate minds come to be thought of as one thing, an audience – will be specially at work. It is not a matter of ingratiation, but in the end the whole thing does depend on the invisible lines of contact that either complete the event or not. Sometimes there seems no way, and the actor making his series of rapid choices on the stage feels he has never hit on the ones that will deliver Shakespeare's man to the public. But he may be wrong, and above all the play is always there, the next day or the next year (when somebody else will be struggling with the problem). Meanwhile we go back to the beginning each time, hopeful not to waste.

A man with a sword comes upon his enemy, whom he has sworn to destroy, at prayer. The promised act of revenge can at this point be performed with relatively little difficulty – indeed with no greater fear of discovery than that of the praying man on an earlier occasion when he destroyed *his* enemy in an orchard. With exultation the armed man approaches his victim and raises his sword.

At this point we stop and see where we are. There is no question in the mind of the spectator but that the sword will certainly come down on the neck of the praying man with all the fury with which it was raised. There is also no question in the mind of the armed man but that he will now do the deed – no question at all. Most oddly of all, in the mind of the actor personifying the man with the sword there is a momentary certainty that tonight will be different, and that his colleague on the floor is about to suffer a severe and unexpected injury.

The alarming question arises: who is actually in charge? If the actor himself is in doubt, then who is masterminding the event and guiding us towards the next action? Everyone waits, the spectators, the two men, the two actors playing the two men, all held for a moment on the same edge, holding the same breath.

Needless to say, things don't always go so sweetly, and I do not mean to mystify. But perhaps it is on hinges such as this that this formidable play finally swings. Certainly all our planning, decisions conscious and unconscious, hunches, strategies and jumps in the dark would add up to very little if they did not in the end lead to just such a small moment of suspense.

Timon of Athens

RICHARD PASCO

RICHARD PASCO, an Associate Artist of the Royal Shakespeare Company, joined the Company in 1969. He had already gained extensive experience in repertory at Birmingham, in London seasons, at the Bristol Old Vic, and on world tours, playing such varied leading roles as Hamlet, Peer Gynt and Jimmy Porter. Outside the theatre, he has established a reputation through his work in television and radio, his many recordings of poetry and plays, and his lecture and recital tour of American universities. His work for the Royal Shakespeare Company has been equally varied, ranging from Polixenes, Leantio in *Women Beware Women*, Proteus in the Theatregoround *Two Gentlemen of Verona* and Buckingham in *Henry VIII* (all in his first season), through the performances of *Richard II* in 1973–4, in which he and Ian Richardson alternated the parts of Richard and Bolingbroke, to his interpretation of the title role in *Timon of Athens* in 1980. This production, designed by Chris Dyer and directed by Ron Daniels, played in repertoire in The Other Place, before closing in 1981.

I had the pleasure of being invited to return to the Royal Shakespeare Company to portray Timon of Athens in the summer of 1980. The part had attracted me since I had been involved as a small-part actor in Sir Tyrone Guthrie's production at the Old Vic in 1952, with André Morell in the title role. The stage was filled with Guthrie's swirling banners and crowds, where every minor character was made to feel as important as the leading protagonists and every facial expression and gesture of a supernumerary as revealing as the agony of Lear in the storm; Guthrie's genius turned Timon's banqueting hall into part of a very heavily populated palace – crowded with courtiers, senators and masquers.

But now I was to play the part of Timon in a production at the Royal Shakespeare Company's small-stage theatre – The Other Place – and

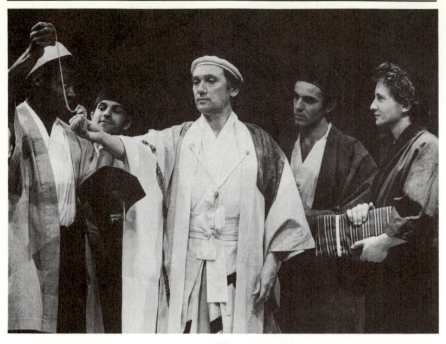

22   'Sir your jewel
        Hath suffered under praise'
                    Richard Pasco as Timon, August 1980

subsequently in Newcastle upon Tyne, in the Gulbenkian Studio, and at the Warehouse in London, with a minimal budget and a cast of some fourteen or so actors; and the problems placed in front of the cast, the director, Ron Daniels, and the designer, Chris Dyer, seemed perhaps infelicitous.

This is probably not the place to discuss the greater or lesser values of a confined acting area with close audience contact and limited material properties and costumes, but with confidence in my director and his designer born of a particularly remarkable production of *Pericles* in similar circumstances a season or so earlier, I welcomed the idea of embarking on the two hours' traffic of *Timon* – this still-born twin of *Lear* – in an intimate situation which would enhance the closer interpretation of the text to the audience, and enable us, we hoped, to overcome the pitfalls of earlier productions of the play, which has been described by various critics over the years as 'unsatisfactory', 'unwieldy', 'authorship disputable', 'unfinished', etc., etc.

The purpose of these reflections is to try to show as much as is possible on paper some of the ideas, or to hint at the conflicts, rehearsal processes, and precepts that face the actors, designer and director who try to bring this play to life by public performance, this play that is to me a grossly neglected masterpiece of dramatic exploration of man's inhumanity to man, and a subtle exposition of the outward manifestations of the human psyche under stress – disillusionment, despair and grief – resulting in a total weariness of body and spirit, culminating in Timon's reconciliation with his maker and whatever lies beyond: 'My long sickness of health and living now begins to mend; and *nothing* brings me all things.' What weariness lay in the heart of our greatest writer when he gave his actor these lines to speak?

I am not able to dissect the structure of the play, nor academically qualified enough to be able to present a finished treatise to you. This can be found in the many excellent essays, critiques and introductions to the play in many varied editions and by scholars such as Wilson Knight, Kenneth Muir and Muriel Bradbrook, but for me, the actor, this has been one of the most completely rewarding and satisfying parts to play in my career, receiving from both audience and critics alike a feeling of compassion for Timon's despair and misanthropy not far removed from the awareness of many individuals existing in our so-called civilized society of the 1980s.

Scholars argue about where, in the Shakespearean canon, *Timon* actually belongs. Suffice to say here that it is almost certainly a late play, post *King Lear* and written within a few years of *The Winter's Tale* and *The Tempest*. The scene is set in Athens and the woods nearby. The principal characters apart from Timon are the soldier Alcibiades, the philosopher Apemantus, and Timon's faithful steward Flavius. We see the rest collectively as faces in a crowd – senators and lords, a poet, a painter and a jeweller; and the only women to appear in the play are masquers at Timon's first banquet, and the mistresses to Alcibiades – Phrynia and Timandra.

The character of the 'noble Athenian', Timon of Athens, is at once a mystery. Shakespeare gives us no hint of his background or his forebears. In most of the great tragedies we know something of the character and background of the leading protagonist, for instance Hamlet's life in Elsinore, Lear's court and his three daughters, Caesar and the state of Rome; but of Timon – nothing. How he acquired his vast wealth and his lands – by inheritance or gift even – there is no mention except: 'To Lacedaemon did my land extend . . .' (2.1.155). We know nothing of wife, sons or daughters, father or mother. He is, of all Shakespeare's major figures, the most alone.

We learn something of him from the Poet and the Painter in the very first scene of the play, as the senators cross the stage and go in to see Timon. The Poet and the Painter act as a kind of chorus of introduction (1.1.38–63).

Timon is revered and adulated. The air is filled with the blandishments of Poet, Painter, Jeweller and senator alike. Later in the play Alcibiades tells Timon:

> I have heard, and grieved,
> How cursed Athens, mindless of thy worth,
> Forgetting thy great deeds when neighbour states,
> But for thy sword and fortune, trod upon them . . .   (4.3.93–6)

And Timon himself says, when asking his faithful steward to go to the senate to borrow money to pay his debtors:

> Go you, sir, to the senators –
> Of whom, even to the state's best health, I have
> Deserved this hearing – bid 'em send o' th' instant
> A thousand talents to me.   (2.2.196–9)

So it is possible that he has been a great benefactor to the state or, indeed, a soldier of some renown. Beyond this we can only surmise.

Timon is not only the plot of the play, but the whole structure would appear to be built around his character. There is neither conflict between hero and heroine, nor between hero and villain; the conflict lies in Timon's inner soul and his response to the betrayal and insults of his friends. It is therefore easy to dismiss Timon's unending generosity as misguided or downright foolish, but his belief in the gift of friendship is from the heart (1.2.88–108); in this speech is the core of the first half of the play: friend–friendship, the obligations of giving, gratitude (and later ingratitude), all in juxtaposition to Timon's question to Apemantus; 'What hast *thou* given? / They never flattered thee . . .' (4.3.270–1). One of my problems in rehearsal was the comparatively little text concerned with the antithetical passions: the passion and urgency of *giving* in the first half of the play, with only brief scenes in which to convey this instinctive munificence, in order to justify, later, the free-ranging misanthropy which makes up the bulk of the latter part of the play, virtually from 3.4.78 (*Enter Timon in a rage*) until the end.

The fascinating character Apemantus – surely a cousin of Jaques and Thersites – the professional cynic, comments on the possible and bitter truth about Timon's flatterers in his asides to the audience in the first act, and indeed to Timon's face (a stage convention easier to manage in an intimate auditorium): 'I scorn thy meat; 'twould choke me, for I should ne'er *flatter* thee . . .' (1.2.38–9). But then, is not Timon's own dispensing of gifts, perhaps, to be seen as a little excessive?

> I take all and your several visitations
> So kind to heart, 'tis not enough to give;
> Methinks I could deal kingdoms to my friends,
> And ne'er be weary.   (1.2.218–21)

His main characteristic is that he is a man with a feeling of enormous compassion towards his fellow human beings – and he is at once, therefore, highly sensitive and greatly vulnerable. Dr Johnson saw the play as 'a moral play, showing the dangers of ostentatious liberality'. For Swinburne, Timon was a 'Christ-like figure of the pre-christian era, whose main characteristic is his nobility'. So the actor's task in the first two and a half acts is the presentation of a dual personality. There is to begin with a noble, passionate human being, who remains alone, but seemingly at peace with himself and the world. But there must be, perhaps, from the start an element of imbalance of personality to justify the split manifested in his behaviour at the second banquet, bringing the ferocity of disillusion, the antithetical hatred of mankind. The psychology of misanthropy was therefore part and parcel of my study of the role's first phase.

The next progression in the play is the steward's continual warnings to his master that his assets are nil, culminating in Timon's confrontation with the creditors after a day's hunting with Alcibiades, and the resulting scene of Timon being told bluntly by the steward that he is bankrupt even to the extent of all his lands being sold. With total ingenuousness he sends his servants to borrow from his friends, convincing his steward that he has nothing to fear. There follows a series of scenes of sardonic humour, where each friend is shown in his true colours – not one of them responds to Timon's pleas, and the servants return empty-handed.

The elusive character and indeed, perhaps, sincerest friend of Timon, Alcibiades, the Athenian Captain, has by now disappeared from the main stream of the play; there is the vital scene in the senate, where his pleas for mercy on a military friend condemned to death result in conviction for the soldier and banishment for Alcibiades; but we do not see him again until he meets Timon by chance in the second half of the play. And so again Timon is alone, save for his faithful steward and the servants who prepare the dishes of lukewarm water and stones that Timon hurls at his fellow senators in the second banquet scene. This public demonstration of contempt is preceded by Timon's prayer to the gods, the 'Grace' said in the presence of the unctuous senators (3.6.69–81), which reveals the beginnings of Timon's *volte face* and his mental breakdown. Across the hair's breadth line between love and hate, a noble innocence is unbalanced, and the play becomes the tragedy of betrayal.

There follows the disintegration of the supposed 'banquet' and the senators retire, bemused, resentful and wet; then Timon's first great soliloquy as he looks back at the walls of Athens and condemns the city and all within to ineffable ruin. This speech in its ferocity and anger is quite equal to anything that Shakespeare wrote for Lear on the blasted heath, and is filled with a kind of cosmic doom that can leave an audience feeling very uneasy indeed (4.1.1–40). The true affection of Timon's steward is again revealed in the following scene as he shares his few pieces of money with two or three other loyal servants of Timon's, and goes off in search of his master (4.2.42–50). We next see Timon, as Shakespeare indicates, in the woods. But these woods, one feels, are never far from the sea. It's a barren coast, filled almost as Prospero's island with strange noises, but beasts and birds of prey abound. From this point onwards there are frequent references to the elements and to the earth, the sun, the moon and the sea. From here to the end of the play the actor's problem is to prevent each set scene from becoming one long shouting-match between Timon and his visitors in the wilderness. This is where Ron Daniels's vision of the 'journey' through the latter half of the play was of most help and inspiration to me, the actor. The play presents the actor with a path towards a journey of redemption – because Timon, seemingly, has never been able to make any genuine human contact, we now see the man revealed by misfortune, not transformed by it. As Professor Muriel Bradbrook states in her greatly helpful work, *The Tragic Pageant of 'Timon of Athens'*: 'This role touches the very frontiers of the articulate, the borders of what can be known of the state of dereliction where conflicts are revealed so deep and elemental, so painful and relatively inaccessible, that only through the most highly established form can they be projected in words as tragic exile. Timon retreats deep in a wintry world, a cinder world; it is winter not only in his purse but in his heart.'

And it is in this stage of the 'journey', through the long third scene of the fourth act, that Shakespeare's genius shows itself in our own time – so much that reflects on our own society and the state of the world of the eighties. As Timon desperately searches for food, Shakespeare's supreme sense of irony reveals itself. Digging frantically for roots, Timon quite by chance discovers a hoard of gold at the very moment of his renunciation of it, an abundance of gold! And the speech against gold is readily seen as an indictment of our own society: the acquisition of more and more, the underlying worthlessness of so much of today's virulent commerce (4.3.34–42). The anger and frustration thrust upon us as, almost like troglodytes, we sit today in front of television, as I have done, watching news bulletins, advertisements and athletes racing for gold. This is Timon's state. His dawning realization of the state of his world – and the cry to Apemantus: 'What wouldst thou do with the World, Apemantus, if it lay in thy power?' – is the clarion call of the individual's helplessness.

Any critic who says that this character is predictable, and doesn't grow or mature, has never, surely, had more than a cursory glance at the text, or even begun to probe Shakespeare's powers of expression of man's bitterness, anger and despair. Leigh Hunt said of Alcibiades' encounter with Timon that it is the meeting of hope with despair; and indeed it is interesting perhaps not only for Timon's rejection of Alcibiades, but also for his reactions to sexual corruption. Timon bids the whores Phrynia and Timandra 'spread disease to youth and mankind alike', as he fills their aprons with gold:

> Consumptions sow
> In hollow bones of man, strike their sharp shins,
> And mar men's spurring. Crack the lawyer's voice,
> That he may never more false title plead,
> Nor sound his quillets shrilly; hoar the flamen,
> That scolds against the quality of flesh
> And not believes himself. Down with the nose,
> Down with it flat; take the bridge quite away
> Of him that, his particular to foresee,
> Smells from the general weal. Make curled-pate ruffians bald,
> And let the unscarred braggarts of the war
> Derive some pain from you.   (4.3.151–62)

The war is the one that Alcibiades is to unleash upon Timon's Athens, that by 'killing of villains' he is to conquer the country. After an invocation to the earth, 'the common whore of mankind', to yield him roots, Timon takes a further step towards regression, and Apemantus enters, spurred on to find Timon because 'Men report that thou dost affect my manners and dost use them.' One can perhaps hear Jaques, Shakespeare's other sour cynic, saying 'Out of these convertites there is much matter to be heard and learned', but Shakespeare puts into Apemantus's mouth that most painful truism, 'The middle of humanity thou never knewest, but the extremity of

23 'What beast couldst thou be that were not subject to a beast?'

both ends' (4.3.300–1). There follows a beautiful scene of point and counterpoint between the professional truculent cynic Apemantus and the desperate Timon, and after Timon's despairing question and the philosopher's curt reply, 'Give it the beasts, to be rid of the men', a speech of supreme denunciation (4.3.327–45). Then the scene ends with abuse hurled from the one to the other and Timon's invocation to the gold scattered at his feet to destroy mankind (4.3.381–96). Bandits and thieves appear and Timon bids them 'Do villainy, do' as he proffers handfuls of gold to the bemused criminals. We transposed the first epitaph passage (4.3.375–80), making it the dawning realization of inner despair after the thieves departed:

> I am sick of this false world, and will love nought
> But even the mere necessities upon't.
> Then, Timon, presently prepare thy grave;
> Lie where the light foam of the sea may beat
> Thy grave-stone daily; make thine epitaph,
> That death in me at others' lives may laugh.

And so Timon begins a period of transition, into a kind of spiritual abnegation. The faithful steward appears and attempts in a profoundly moving scene to persuade Timon to let him stay and comfort him, but after a scene of implacable benevolence, Timon banishes the steward having proffered handfuls of gold to him with the injunction:

> Go, live rich and happy,
> But thus condition'd: thou shalt build from men;
> Hate all, curse all, show charity to none,
> But let the famish'd flesh slide from the bone
> Ere thou relieve the beggar. Give to dogs
> What thou deniest to men. Let prisons swallow 'em,
> Debts wither 'em to nothing; be man like blasted woods,
> And may diseases lick up their false bloods!
> And so farewell and thrive. (4.3.525–33)

Timon then commences to write his epitaph. There are no stage directions as to when and how this is performed. After some pause for this purpose, the Poet and Painter reappear to seek gold once again from the bounteous Timon; he drives them out in a fit of rage and mockery. The play draws towards its conclusion with the faithful steward reappearing with two of the senators who try to appeal to Timon to return to Athens and protect them from the onslaught of Alcibiades and his army; we, as audience, know that Timon has passed beyond worldly hate and misanthropy, to an almost trance-like willingness for death:

My long sickness
Of health and living now begins to mend,
And nothing brings me all things.   (5.1.186–8)

He repels the senators in one last scene of acute melancholic humour and irony, and prepares for death – in the most conclusive lines uttered by any of Shakespeare's major tragic figures:

Lips, let four words go by and language end:
What is amiss, plague and infection mend!
Graves only be men's works and death their gain.
Sun, hide thy beams, Timon hath done his reign.   (5.1.220–3)

We are left uncertain as to *how* Timon dies. Shakespeare writes only *Exit*. It is remarkable that of all Shakespeare's tragic heroes Timon is the only one to walk from the stage instead of being carried from it. Does he drown, or starve, in his cave, or on the sea-shore? Is his death by natural causes, or in the final despair, by his own hand? We do not know what Shakespeare intended. We solved the problem by having Timon draw a net over himself by the sea's edge.

Sir Arthur Quiller-Couch said he was 'content simply to wonder at the miracle of Shakespeare and to leave to critics the task of explaining him'. It is left to Alcibiades to read the epitaph on Timon's tomb:

Here lies a wretched corse, of wretched soul bereft;
Seek not my name; a plague consume you, wicked caitiffs left!
Here lie I, Timon, who, alive, all living men did hate;
Pass by and curse thy fill, but pass and stay not here thy gait.

                                                        (5.4.70–3)

Shakespeare's masterpiece about the vulnerability of mankind, the mortal sickness at the core of life, ends with the coda spoken by Alcibiades, as he enters in vengeance and triumph into Timon's city, Athens:

Dead
Is noble Timon, of whose memory
Hereafter more. Bring me into your city,
And I will use the olive with my sword,
Make war breed peace, make peace stint war, make each
Prescribe to other, as each other's leech.
Let our drums strike.   (5.4.79–85)

Posthumus in
Cymbeline

ROGER REES

ROGER REES, an Associate Artist of the Royal Shakespeare Company, joined the Company for the 1968 season, after early and varied experience in repertory. In Stratford, he first played minor parts in plays which took him, in 1970, to the Aldwych and on tours to Japan and Australia. The following year he was Claudio (*Much Ado*) and Roderigo; and he has since broadened his range, both in Shakespeare – in 1976 alone, he appeared at the two Stratford theatres as Antipholus of Syracuse, Benvolio, Malcolm, and the Young Shepherd in *The Winter's Tale* – and in such other plays as *The Way of the World* and *The Three Sisters*. In 1980 he played the title role in the now famous production of *Nicholas Nickleby*, winning for his performance the Society of West End Theatre Award for Best Actor in 1980, and, after the season in the United States, the New York Tony Award for Best Actor in 1981. He returned to Stratford in 1984 to play Hamlet. He played Posthumus Leonatus in 1979 to Judi Dench's Imogen in the production of *Cymbeline* directed by David Jones, with Christopher Morley as designer.

When a director asks me to consider playing a certain part, especially one from the classical repertoire, my mind's eye – long before the request has been completed – presents my brain with a visual image of myself in successful performance, and in this private movie-show I'm doing famously. As the offer is made my senses leap to recognize the shape of the sound of the name of the character and, in a milli-second of industry, they chip out a figure; underneath this activity my deeper conscience is flicking through the card-index of actors who have played the part previously, leaving free a bump of my intellect to work out chances in the slips. This bright, quick vision is a flash of glory and achievement, and in it I am craft and praise and golden. I am choice. The bubble bursts when once I admit

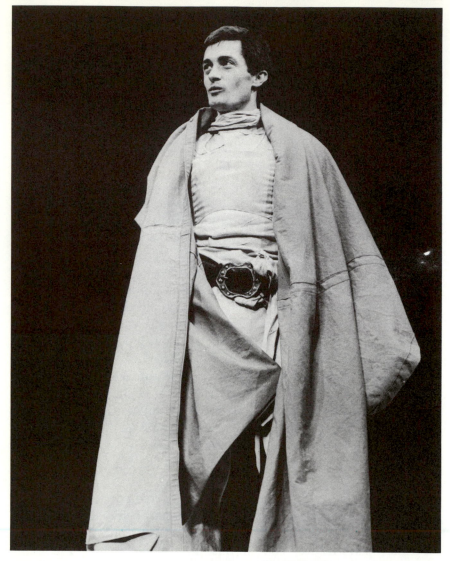

24   'I will remain
The loyal'st husband that did e'er plight troth'
Roger Rees as Posthumus, April 1979

to being interested in the proposal, '. . . well, yes, look here, I could have a stab at it . . . [pause] . . . I suppose I should wait to say that till the time you offer me Macbeth, but still . . . yes, I think that I'd like to have a go . . .' From the delightful yet brief fantasy of playing a part exceedingly well, a marvellous though involuntary mirage of acclaim and possibility, one must fall, and it's a stumbling trip down-stage to sharp reality; a Richard-out-of-Flint descent to darkness, harness and toil, to the first painful steps in fleshing out a character.

Eventually, after work which no one outside a theatre could possibly understand, or be the remotest bit interested in, one might make the role ring and shine for an audience; but for the actor the character can never be as beautiful again.

When I was offered this part for the season at Stratford-upon-Avon in 1979, David Jones, the director and a man with whom I'd worked a lot before, said these alchemical words: 'If you fancy it, old chum, we'd . . . well, in reality, *I'd* be very pleased if you'd think of having a bash at that old misogynist Posthumus Leonatus, bloody fool that he is . . .' How could I resist this silver-tongued charm bracelet? My mind soared with the idea of the part; pushing any thought of labour aside, I saw Posthumus flying. All the tiny stored informations that I'd nurtured about the character flew within my memory and flapped about my brain. I recall what I recalled: Posthumus, firstly, is Britain and virtue personified, Jupiter's boy eagle with talon and red-eye, polite at first to foreigners, but secretly sure that dogs begin at Calais. In his prejudice he is no flyer but earthy and proud, shaggy and tawny-maned, an uncivil braggadocio. In Britain the very man for love but in Rome, out of his depth in very hot water, he becomes a spoilt boy lost, longing for mother country and her apron strings to cling to. In vengeance against his supposedly faithless wife he is steely and irrational by turns, too much in love to care and too careful to love with loyalty, and his eventual regret blinds him to any sort of truthfulness or reason, as he sets himself for death and nothing less. I suppose that a man with his upbringing could never accept that he had been wrong-footed by an Italian ('Italian fiend! Ay me, most credulous fool'), it would be *too* unthinkable. I imagined Posthumus as everything the world has come to expect of the true-born Englishman. Posthumus, duped and lonely, missed his young wife, stuck at a traffic-jam between invasions waiting for Douglas Bader to be born and cricket to be invented. Poor Leonatus, just a hero, not man. This cardboard cut-out version of the chap made me want to play him. I wanted to have a go at explaining his infuriatingly inexplicable behaviour.

I thought him stupid and dull and spiteful and I wanted to see why; I challenged myself to believe that I might find some unifying aspect in his nature to forgive the cruel disparity in his emotions. Just as a word of very few letters will solve a puzzle, I sought a simple key to the enigma that is Imogen's husband; her twin, the masculine journey of her soul.

I can readily understand why as an actor I was attracted to the character's plainness and lack of sparkle; for some time I'd been cornering the market in chaps unheroic, blokes like Roderigo in *Othello* – I'd tried to make him real enough for an audience to believe that he might deserve Desdemona even though he was only (my scenario, this) the assistant librarian in the Army Catering Corps in Venice. As for Gratiano in *The Merchant of Venice*, I attempted to make some equation between his nervously loud mouth and his loyalty (this experiment frightened the general public, the horses, and the critics); and Aguecheek in *Twelfth Night*, raven-haired for once, 'it hangs *like* flax on a distaff'; and, most recently, Baron Tusenbach in Tchekov's *Three Sisters*, uncontrollably in love with Irena unto death. All these characters fail, either in life or as personalities. But I was attracted to them as men who are lucky enough to glimpse, each of them, one small inch of mastery in their lives; all find a tiny moment of decorum and dignity that they never expected they were capable of. I was doing pretty well with these people, and had settled myself into a cuddly middle-aged version of myself, looking forward to being a definitive Horatio to somebody's Great Dane, and setting my secret sights, by way of a pension scheme, on Gayev in *The Cherry Orchard* when I became sixty-five.

I suppose I was a little flattered by being offered Posthumus, there is something so athletically pliant about his image – its heroic scope, I suppose – that I had never thought to tackle. The famous lament of women in our profession, that by the time you are old enough to understand Juliet you are too matronly to play her, holds good for the men as well; and though the 'old man' Frank Benson went on giving Romeo well into his sixties, one must be cautious; 'Hamlet, Prince of Stretchmark' is a terrifying part to play.

Was there more then to this birdman of Albion, this twin to Imogen, than his theatrical unpopularity allowed? Could his journey through the play, a brave man but dull, passing love and hatred and reaching atonement through the clumsiest of roads, be made to move an audience? Might his unwieldy, illogical and unfashionable jingoistic tale be brought to seem as important to the play's climax of peace and forgiveness as that of Imogen herself? Posthumus in recent productions, I discovered, is usually pared down to the very minimum; David Jones offered me a very full text to play, and so I decided to jump in headlong with both eyes tightly shut and try to imbue the part with the significance that so moves me in other lost and losing partners in Shakespeare's work, as Sebastian, Pericles or Leontes.

So I had a reason for wanting to play the part. A great believer in *need* in the theatre, I think that if you don't want to or don't need to play a part sufficiently much, or, indeed, lack a real direction about why you want to mount a production, then you must step aside and allow someone who has a more urgent need, to have a go. I cannot claim to have always had such purpose, and, of course, I cannot know whether such zeal will stay with me; I hope it does, it's a freeing and demanding freshening thing to experience day by day in the theatre.

My need was to find the man inside the hero, inside the words of the script that made up the hero's thoughts and actions, so that when I came to perform him I could be a man first and foremost, and a warrior and saviour later – a being who happened to be brave at times and frail at others, just as people are. Shakespeare had done the work, I had no doubt of that, and it was just my ignorance and lack of humility that prevented my decoding the charm. As I set to work on the text I tried, hard as I could, to strip away my preconceptions of the part and the play. I had trained not for the stage but for the fine arts and at moments such as these I have great struggle to put things visual from me and to replace them with considerations more intelligent than that Posthumus should have an eagle tattooed on his chest.

Trying to read any sort of play is difficult enough; you have to hold in your head a tally of all those other characters who have chosen not to speak but are still on stage. A character who doesn't speak in Shakespeare is sometimes much more significant and illuminating to the plot than one who gabbles on and on. At least that's what I believed when I played the eighth lord in *As You Like It*. Reading an Elizabethan or Jacobean text is pretty tricky, and reading it as though you have never met the piece before is almost impossible. But if an actor is to tell a story, freshly, then preconceptions and bias must be eliminated. If I knew nothing of *Romeo and Juliet* and the sources of the story, what shock and sadness there would be for me in Juliet's awakening in the Capulets' tomb. How wonderful and just that the statue of Hermione should come to life in *The Winter's Tale*, but how much I would give not to expect it. A wilderness of monkeys, of course, and a season ticket to the London Zoo, not to know the news that Tubal brings to Shylock, that the actor might tease me through his alternating grief and rage. Does Shakespeare mention a balcony? Why shouldn't Othello be a short swift man rather like Haile Selassie? Why Romeo good-looking? Why should Beatrice and Benedick be youthful? Is the impenetrable 'dram of ill' in *Hamlet* merely a record of Burbage busking till the actor playing the Ghost (Shakespeare, probably) made good his late entrance? Is Macbeth's shout to 'Ring the alarum bell!' a reminder to the sound-effect department, a stage direction or part of the text? Why is Posthumus so very humourless and dull?

The Kembles and the Keans and the Macreadys used, I believe, to amuse themselves in their lighter hours with Posthumus, but he can scarcely be said to be first-rate sport – there is even less to be done with him than with Iachimo.

History is never meant to be a comfort; this is Henry James writing in *Harper's Weekly* in 1896 and reviewing *Cymbeline* in Irving's production at the Lyceum Theatre in London. As the first rehearsals approached my research on the subject of Posthumus Leonatus accelerated, and my time for running the mile on the athletics track in Battersea Park diminished; my body and mind were moving from sloth to stimulation. The part of Posthumus, I discovered, contains many a soliloquy. I realized that I had never, except for four lines as a very febrile Claudio in *Much Ado About Nothing*, spoken alone on a stage in my life. Did the management realize this?, I said to myself.

When you audition for a classical company it is thought a good idea to have prepared two pieces, one ancient and one modern; when I auditioned for the RSC many years ago I delivered my two soliloquies so nervously that I'm certain it was impossible to differentiate one from the other. 'Thank you, Mr Rees. That was, "Oh God, methinks it were a happy life", from *Henry the Sixth*, part three.' 'Oh no, I'm sorry. That was Stanley from *The Birthday Party*.' 'Oh yes, of course it was. . . . Well, thank you.' These auditions were my last soliloquies, and therefore at rehearsals I was pretty shy and diffident, nursing a blind panic and individual terror for later on.

For the first days of rehearsal we sat around talking pie in the sky and castles in Milford Haven, not wishing to admit to each other how very difficult this last great poem was going to prove. Ellen Terry held my hand for comfort, or rather Judi Dench did (the same thing, really). In 1896 Imogen was played by Miss Terry, her natural charm and gaiety making it inevitable for Irving that the piece should be attempted; in 1979 the Imogen was Judi Dench and our production started out with an exactly similar premise. Henry James might well have been writing of Judi Dench's final performance in this review of Ellen Terry (he is unusually sympathetic, he generally disliked her acting):

Her immense naturalness throughout the character is of the highest value, through its enabling her to throw all her powers, without any of the arts usually employed to that end, into the positive innocence of it – that of the young wife youthfully in love with her absent husband. The impulsiveness of this innocence breaking out in confident high spirits, draws, by its vivid opposition to the evil that is believed of her, the one happy effect that can be drawn from the foolish story of the husband's instantaneous surrender. But everything in *Cymbeline* is instantaneous – doubt and faith, love and hate, recognition and despair, damnation and forgiveness, victory and defeat, – everything.

With faith, love, recognition and forgiveness in the very capable hands of the Misses Terry and Dench, I felt I'd drive myself hard to get to the 'evil that is believed of her'. People have reacted to the play down the centuries as positively as James did. I found this interesting and helpful. Either the play was loved, a late great poem, a master daring to depart from his accepted forms, or the play was dismissed as historical bunkum, with some concession made to the nice little song in Act 4. More importantly than this, I noticed that the character of Posthumus elicited a similarly disparate response. In some commentaries he was considered and discussed, in some he was immediately written off as being impossible to play or even talk about; most often, he was not mentioned at all. I realized, of course, that the part wasn't Richard II, but was he just a 'feed' to Iachimo? Had I been sold a pup?

As rehearsals moved from London to Stratford my hold on reality and confidence moved further from me as the first night loomed nearer. I threw myself back at the text in the comparative calm of Warwickshire, and tried not to ignore but to encompass all the violently changing traits of Posthumus into one complete being. Wig calls interrupted my rehearsing and my reading; I thought that Leonatus should have hair like a lion, short and cadet-like in the first two acts, and then on his return from exile, a changed man, no longer a boy but Charles Bronson himself, hair Periclean! I wanted a great red mane of hair and a beard to match; when the costume arrived, a sort of short leathern cocktail dress, I let the wig go. I left them to it and went back to my books.

I found the strange disparity in his nature mentioned again in an unidentified review of Charles Kemble at Covent Garden in 1820:

Macready's Iachimo was a fine performance, full of Italian subtlety and Roman strength, and was greatly applauded. This was probably the chief character of the play, and he went through it with a due sense of importance. Kemble's Posthumus had the grace, the purity and the interest of his habitual style, but Posthumus palters too doubtfully between affection and revenge, is too lightly deceived and is too severe in vindication of his honour to be a favourite.

145

I was starting to find Posthumus's paltering attractive and his swiftly violent swoop from faith to utter disgust almost hypnotic. Perhaps I was wrong not to see the character as a fool and his actions as ridiculous? Perhaps no one with Posthumus's upbringing could be anything but spoilt and ever so faintly amusing? I went back to the first scene of the play. There I realized that poor Posthumus had so much to live up to that he had to take a tumble, sooner or later. Being famous at too early an age is a gift that only the most resilient prodigy can handle:

FIRST GENTLEMAN   The king he takes the babe
To his protection; calls him Posthumus Leonatus,
Breeds him, and makes him of his bedchamber:
Puts to him all the learnings that his time
Could make him the receiver of; which he took
As we do air, fast as 'twas minister'd;
And in his spring became a harvest: liv'd in court
(Which rare it is to do) most prais'd, most lov'd:
A sample to the youngest, to the more mature,
A glass that feated them: and to the graver,
A child that guided dotards: to his mistress
For whom he now is banish'd, – her own price
Proclaims how she esteem'd him and his virtue;
By her election may be truly read
What kind of man he is.
SECOND GENTLEMAN   I honour him
Even out of your report.   (1.1.40–55)

At last I started to see Posthumus as a dupe and amusing! This was such a breakthrough for me – I started to get a sense of the ridiculous, which leads to fondness and eventual redemption in characters so stiff. Posthumus should have done but he didn't; he didn't think twice about marrying Imogen, the heir to the British throne; he did not conceive of the danger presented by the new Queen; and, as companion and playfellow to the King's daughter, brought up as himself a prince – a king's son in everything but blood – what would he think more natural than taking her to his wife? Banished in his first scene from everything he has been encouraged to hold close, his wife, his country, his foster-father, this man can be a golden prince no longer; Snow White will die with a bite of the poisoned apple and no prince to comfort her; Posthumus's final words in his first scene, the last time we see Imogen with her husband, are 'I am gone!' This phrase rings schizophrenically in the air. Whatever happens, he can be the 'most prais'd, most lov'd' no more.

Garrick earned great success as Posthumus, though I suspect that he tampered with the play to give his own ends the means; Macready preferred Iachimo, as Irving did, interestingly enough, in his revival for Ellen Terry. Ben Kingsley, 'my' Iachimo, was doing famously in 1979, nipping in and out of the trunk in the bedroom to much joy and applause in rehearsal and – this last giving me pause and stirring not a little envy – laughter. I think that if there has got to be a secret to playing any hero then it is that one ought to be able to get a laugh or two out of him – not at him but *with* him. The continuing presence in Shakespeare's work is humour and ironic observation; they are to be teased from the dourest and sourest of parts. Bushy, Bagot and Green, for instance, were the veritable Wilson, Keppel and Betty of 1597, and Clyde Pollitt even managed to strangle a couple of titters out of the gaoler who meets the ready-for-death Post-humus in this production – though, of course, Mr Pollitt was the actor who swears that, when he made his final exit as Puss-in-Boots in Christmas pantomime in Newcastle in the 1950s, the audience immediately set up a chant of 'Bring back the cat! Bring back the cat!'

But to the more serious business of laughter. The speech that forms Act 2, Scene 5, I found very difficult until I started to unfold the humour of it. It was not until the very late rehearsals when David Jones managed to persuade me that my ridiculous endearment, my over-patriotically zealous love and my protest-too-much hatred as the character were beginning to make the man, that I ventured strongly. I was still very scared of these soliloquies; staring your peers in the eye in the open light of a rehearsal-room is so much more demanding than the comfort of an anonymous audience in a darkened auditorium. You come face to face in fellow actors with yourself, and as they understand your inadequacies so very well (they have them themselves), you have nowhere to hide save in truly attempting the character. I can recall David Threlfall, Smike to my Nicholas Nickleby in a later extravaganza, sitting quietly, interested in what I was doing at a rehearsal as a fellow actor, but putting me off so badly that I packed up and stalked off home, wounded. It wasn't his fault but mine; the act of making a character is a delicate thing, there are no rules; it showed me that I was still uncertain and hadn't found Posthumus's true centre. David Jones was trying to push me to play this speech (2.5) as rawly and as plainly as possible; the scene provides the bridge for the character across the next two acts in which he does not appear, almost two hours' playing-time in the theatre, enough time for an audience to forget the man completely. David tried to make me see the speech as truly amusing in its context; certainly deeply sad, and yet very ironic; a line from David

Edgar's adaptation of Dickens's *Nicholas Nickleby* comes to my mind: Miss Knag, who has been usurped in her position in the show-room at the Mantalini millinery business by Kate Nickleby, asks the girls in the work-room, 'Have I worked here all these years to be called elderly?' Posthumus seems equally to be railing at nature itself with his first lines:

> Is there no way for men to be, but women
> Must be half-workers? (2.5.1–2)

Silly lad, led by the nose into a supposed cuckoldom, he takes it out on heredity and the act of generation: his movement towards reality and a coming out of this petulance with any humanity was very hard for me to trace at this time.

In the scene before this speech we tried to find a locale in which Posthumus and Philario (Leonatus's surrogate Dad) might talk of things political in a relaxed and open manner; we elected to assume that they had just come from taking a Turkish bath (this, not for the first time in a Shakespearean production, I suspect), thus providing a situation in which Iachimo could catch Posthumus at his most vulnerable (i.e., without his trousers on) when he relates his apparent conquest of Imogen's virtue and fidelity. Good symbolic thinking, this. We even discussed at one time whether I should throw in the towel altogether for the speech against women which follows immediately and play it exposed in every respect, a Michelangelo life drawing, a nude in a Francis Bacon painting, the innocent turned Renaissance man by falsehood and guile – empty, lost and naked. In the first scene Posthumus loses wife and country; then makes his vows, too adamant and brittle to be trusted:

> I will remain
> The loyal'st husband that did e'er plight troth. (1.1.95–6)

> You gentle gods, give me but this I have,
> And cere up my embracements from a next
> With bonds of death! Remain, remain thou here,
> *(putting on the ring)*
> While sense can keep it on. (1.1.115–18)

This pompous boy must lose his senses, go mad, desert to deserve Imogen and then be given her again with the realization that he has been stripped of his pretensions. It was a good schematic notion, this nudity, but in the end I wore a pair of Anglo-Saxon boxer-shorts, a consensus of opinion amongst the cast being that I had enough troubles without encouraging more.

Looking at my script I can see the marks that I made in the margins of this speech; there is a lot about 'Devils!' and there is a slight pause marked in 2.5.7 – 'so doth my [*slight pause*] wife' – that I might tell the audience I knew my wife was my wife no longer, which I rejected as harmful to the rhythm. I see I've written that the idea of 'I'll write against them' is 'More IMPORTANT than I think!' His very next action is, of course, apart from putting on some clothes, to write to Pisanio his servant, and to command him to kill Imogen. It's very good to be aware of such letters if you are the character who is supposed to have penned them:

IMOGEN (*reads*) Thy mistress, Pisanio, hath played the strumpet in my bed; the testimonies whereof lies bleeding in me. I speak not out of weak surmises; but from proof as strong as my grief, and as certain as I expect my revenge. That part, thou, Pisanio, must act for me. (3.4.21–6)

I found a great clue in this letter. Iachimo never absolutely stated, only suggested to Posthumus's over-active and childishly fertile imagination, that Imogen had been wanton, and to me it seemed that Posthumus was more worried about his own reputation than by his wife's dishonesty.

IACHIMO   Will you hear more?
POSTHUMUS Spare your arithmetic, never count the turns:
                     Once, and a million!
IACHIMO   I'll be sworn –
POSTHUMUS   No swearing:
                     If you will swear you have not done't you lie,
                     And I will kill thee if thou dost deny
                     Thou'st made me cuckold.
IACHIMO   I'll deny nothing.
POSTHUMUS Oh, that I had her here to tear her limb-meal! (2.4.141–7)

I can remember in performance the delight that Ben Kingsley and I enjoyed in forcing the pentameter through the shared lines. Picking up cues can become most magically truthful when lines are separated between characters. For example:

IACHIMO   Since the true life on't was –
POSTHUMUS   This is true:
                     And this you might have heard of her, by me,
                     Or by some other.
IACHIMO   More particulars
                     Must justify my knowledge.
POSTHUMUS   So they must,
                     Or do your honour injury.
IACHIMO   The chimney
                     Is south the chamber. (2.4.76–81)

Played with speed and a continuous rhythm 'the chimney' fell into the air like a trump card at bridge and exploded a response from the audience.

In Stratford . . . a collision of the Decameron, Holinshed, and Snow-White, with its plot in a mazy damascene, its twenty-four cumulated dénouements in the last act, its verse sometimes obscure, sometimes stained with the murex, and for its heroine Imogen, Shakespeare's nonpareil, who makes us realise why Posthumus said to her 'Hang there like fruit, my soul, till the tree die!' It was baffling to rehearse. The company, at it from early morning on the Birthday, missed the processions and felt rebellious.

No not us, but Frank Benson's company in Stratford in 1909 (described by J. C. Trewin in *Benson and the Bensonians*); the river flows on.

What is this then about humour making a dullard palatable? May we only be redeemed when we have come to terms with our foolishness? Should every good man be able to laugh at himself? Posthumus is no laughing matter, but at 2.4.118–20 I was able to make him change his opinion of Imogen's supposed strumpetry with such a dazzling doggedness that, almost on his behalf, lest he should have to soften his upper lip to do

25 'Gods, put the strength o'th'Leonati in me!'

so, the audience nudged themselves into a little chuckle. This laugh was achieved by no actor's artifice but is inherent in the character's personality. Actors can strive and strive but fail to remember that the audience hold the story, they are the focus. They needed no winking to understand that Posthumus was playing devil's advocate against himself:

POSTHUMUS   Back my ring,
                Render to me some corporal sign about her
                More evident than this: for this was stol'n.
IACHIMO   By Jupiter, I had it from her arm.
POSTHUMUS Hark you, he swears: by Jupiter he swears.
                'Tis true, nay, keep the ring, 'tis true . . .   (2.4.118–23)

It is enough. Posthumus and Imogen were married in the Temple of Jupiter; he must believe it. Everything he is, and has been told he is, instructs him so. The second and last instance reveals how much he changes and how dearly he deserves our attention when he returns to Britain. In 5.3, irritated by a Britain lord's lack of interest in things material, Posthumus, with fine and patriotic anger, lapses into rhyming couplets and, finding himself lapsed, blames the lord for putting him there. This joke two hours and one year and a supposed death later is of Posthumus's own manufacture; he has, thank Jove, discovered irony, and what a step for this dull portrait of plain husbandry!

POSTHUMUS   Lack, to what end?
                Who dares not stand his foe, I'll be his friend:
                For if he'll do as he is made to do,
                I know he'll quickly fly my friendship too.
                You have put me into rhyme!
LORD   Farewell, you're angry! (*Exit*)
POSTHUMUS Still going? This is a lord! Oh, noble misery!   (5.3.59–64)

Now this exchange may have been one small step for Tommy Cooper but it's a giant leap for Posthumus Leonatus. Things for him are no longer black and white, he may not be the Thane of Cawdor, and he's no Henry V, though as I understand it I think that even he would be hard put to come up with something as beautiful as 'noble misery'.

Of course, he's one of those quiet poets who never publish, though I find it interesting that while he fights shy of poeticism in the field, when fettered and in solitary confinement he dreams visions in such antique doggerel as would shame all but the most vehemently sentimental. The part keeps its secrets. This is Macready before he swallowed *his* pride and took to playing Iachimo:

May 18th, 1837. Acted Posthumus (Cymbeline) in a most discreditable manner undigested, unstudied. Oh, it was culpable to hazard so my reputation! I was ashamed of myself.

Was I in the same position? Shakespeare wriggles free whatever we do or do not venture.

Hermione in
The Winter's Tale

GEMMA JONES

G EMMA JONES gained her early experience in repertory, before moving to London. She has been seen all over the world as Titania and Hippolyta in a Royal Shakespeare Company tour of *A Midsummer Night's Dream*, as Lady Macbeth in a Cambridge Theatre Company Indian tour, and in the title role in the television series, *The Duchess of Duke Street*. She came to Stratford in 1981 to play Hermione, and has since appeared at the Barbican as Lady Mortimer in Part 1 and Doll Tearsheet in Part 2 of *Henry IV*; at The Other Place as Lady Politic Would-Be in *Volpone*; and at the Royal Shakespeare Theatre as Maria in *Twelfth Night*, Queen Katherine in *Henry VIII*, and Portia in *Julius Caesar*. Patrick Stewart played Leontes to her Hermione, in a production designed by Chris Dyer and directed by Ronald Eyre.

I am asked to meet . . . with a view to . . . the possibility of . . . the role of Hermione in *The Winter's Tale*. 'You know, the statue one.' Early 1981; I have just returned from a Cambridge Theatre Company tour of India, playing Lady Macbeth. Prior to that I have put both Beatrice and Portia under my belt with a certain degree of professionalism and adequacy. So why, when I am asked to meet with a view to . . . the possibility of . . . the role of Hermione, do I react like a nervous novice? Am I so frightened? Or is it excitement in disguise; the start of another adventure; a wondrous maze and an endless journey into the words of William Shakespeare? In the beginning was the word! I reach for my collected works and turn to *The Winter's Tale*: Hermione – his wife. I attempt to read the play. My anxiety to achieve instant enlightenment into the character of Hermione impedes my understanding. I resort to Charles and Mary Lamb, who tell me a tale:

Leontes, King of Sicily, and his queen, the beautiful and virtuous Hermione, once lived in the greatest harmony together.

And thus barely equipped I keep my appointment to meet the director. I

153

26   'Was not my lord
The verier wag o'th'two?'
Gemma Jones as Hermione with Polixenes (Ray Jewers)
and Leontes (Patrick Stewart), June 1981

camouflage my ignorance with a deal of overt enthusiasm, and assimilate a
feeling of intellectual excitement and commitment from Ronald Eyre who
has preliminary ideas for a production marked by simplicity and boldness
of story-telling. I note down 'The Brothers Grimm' and 'Market day in
Victorian Connemara'. I voice my impression that the production looks
like being a nursery edition of the Bayeux Tapestry – an observation that is
greeted with such enthusiasm that it takes me a long time to dismiss the
idea that I will need a pack of greyhounds straining at the leash and a tame
unicorn to interpret this role. I attempt to subdue my awe at the possibility
of working with the Royal Shakespeare Company and come away
energized and excited at the thought of the task ahead. With some weeks to
go before the start of rehearsals, I wonder where to begin. I query that with
all my years of experience in this work I do not have a defined process of
preliminary investigation. I go to Foyles and buy the *New Shakespeare*
edition – the one with the Picasso sketch on the front. I like that. I reckon
they would have liked each other – Pablo and Will – eating figs and
drinking wine under a Provençal sun.

I write my name in the front and in the back a quote from an interview with Picasso:

I order things in accordance with my passions. What a sad thing for a painter who loves blondes but denies himself the pleasure of putting them in the picture because they don't go well with the basket of fruit. What misery for a painter who detests apples to have to use them all the time to harmonize with the table cloth! I put in my pictures everything I like – So much the worse for the things – they have to get along with one another!

The relevance of this to my task is oblique, but it's brave and it makes me smile. I also underline my speeches and note that Hermione appears in Act 1, Scene 2, Act 2, Scene 1, Act 3, Scene 2, and Act 5, Scene 3; and thus I make a start. I read the play. I reread the play. My antennae are out. My thoughts are upon it, realizing themselves at strange and often inappropriate times. I return home on the no. 24 bus and contemplate sexual jealousy. The bus conductor looks quite nervous. The whole of North London seems to be populated with pregnant women; I wonder that we can feel so unique and miraculous when there are so many of us.

Between now and the first rehearsal the *New Shakespeare* edition becomes familiar to me; its form, its size, its colour, its layout and my illegible scrawls in the margin. When I am subsequently presented with the *New Penguin* Shakespeare I am disproportionately bereft and it takes me some time to convert my allegiance.

I treat the new back page to Plato:

He who without the muses' madness in his soul comes knocking at the door of poesy and thinks that Art will make him anything fit to be called a poet, finds that the poetry which he endites in his sober senses is beaten hollow by the poetry of a mad man.

I attempt to convert my notes from the redundant copy to the new, but can only decipher 'Persil automatic', 'Whiskas', 'loo paper', 'dentist'.

Ron Eyre phones to ask if I would consider being involved in the Bohemia festivities of the second act, possibly as an orange-seller, even maybe walking through the audience. 'Oh! yes please', I say. Instant vision of myself as an extremely voluptuous, if small-breasted, Nell Gwyn, startling the audience with my extraordinary versatility. I read the play. I read Edith Sitwell's notes on *The Winter's Tale* and Margaret Webster's references to the play in *Shakespeare Today*. I find it hard to assimilate their observations at this stage in my awareness. I skirt the issue and sniff around the edges of it.

I look up photographs in my illustrated edition; of Charles Kean as

Leontes and Ellen Terry as Mamillius; Judi Dench who played both Hermione and Perdita in the Royal Shakespeare Company production of 1969; Peggy Ashcroft who played Paulina in 1960 and Ian McKellen who was Leontes in 1976 when my father, Griffith Jones, played Antigonus. I look at the photographs and attempt to glean a flavour of their interpretations. I read the play. I dip into *The Creative Process*, an anthology of writings and interviews with artists. I note down:

'The Singing Chaos of the Unexpected' — John Livingston Lowes

'A State of complete suspense' — Isadora Duncan

'Words belong to the sheltering conception of light and order which is our refuge' — Conrad

'The time for work should be that time when the excited mind moves most free of the encumbrance of its consciously supported order.'

I read the play.

I take my young son to the Bear Gardens Museum and Arts Centre in Southwark, which stands on the original site of the bear-baiting area and Hope Playhouse. I attempt to explain to him with the help of three-dimensional scale models how Shakespeare's plays may have been performed in his time. My son is more interested in gory replicas of beheaded traitors spiked on London Bridge. If, as the preface to my *New Shakespeare* tells me, '*The Winter's Tale* was one of the entertainments supplied for the marriage of Elizabeth of Bohemia to the Elector Palatine in 1613', might it have been played at the Swan or the Rose or the Globe, but a stone's throw from where I now stand? My inclination towards sentimental reverie is abruptly stifled by 'Does it hurt?' 'What?' 'Having your head chopped off?' And it bears little relationship to my earning my living by interpreting the role of Hermione in 1981 – but I get a faded glimpse of a tenuous link with my heritage. 'No, of course not', I say rather nervously, anticipating nightmares. 'And anyway it doesn't happen any more. Now just try to imagine Christopher Wren standing on this spot and watching St Paul's Cathedral being built.'

I have a call for a first rehearsal. 'Fear o'ershades me.' I read the play. First rehearsal. The company meets. Twenty-four actors, the director, the director's assistant, the designer and assorted stage management assemble in the ballroom – a low-ceilinged, inadequately lit, sepulchral space underneath the Notre Dame Church next door to the Prince Charles Cinema in Leicester Square. I arrive with time to spare and am tempted by the photographs of *Caligula* outside the cinema. How much easier to dive in there than into the bowels of the Notre Dame Hall to follow my fate. I smile oh! so gaily, and laugh oh! too much, and latch on to those few that I know, two of whom I was at drama school with too long ago. We have rarely met since, but I find a security in a kind of fraternal familiarity because we were younger together. I sit in a circle of strangers next to Sheila Falkenor who is to be our choreographer. She is also a dancer and a mother. If time could stand just for a bit, we could have a nice chat about two topics that I feel confidently opinionated about.

We begin. We are introduced to one another and twenty-four names are wiped from my mind like chalk from a slate. Ronald Eyre presents his brief. His belief in the play; the complexities of the characters; the intricacies of the verse; symbolism; allegory; Christianity; sin; redemption and the apparently legendary problem of how to connect the two halves of the play – the treacherous but rewarding journey ahead of us.

Stephen Oliver has written a 'Hymn to Apollo' to be sung in five-part harmony by the whole company during the oracle scene and we gather round the piano for an initial introduction. Whether the newly assembled company is endowed with an exceptional musical talent or whether Stephen Oliver's energy sets off a somewhat nervous and frenetic enthusiasm in his cast, the first rendition of his music is startling; and so we take our first corporate step and rehearsals commence.

My reading, reading and rereading of the play have not provided me with an instantly clear vision of Hermione. The words that she speaks, the lines that she says, I comprehend; but her motives are obscure. I suspect that she has no ulterior motive and that she is indeed 'The Good Queen', 'Continent, chaste and true'. I am reluctant to accept it. I resist 'good'. Why? Why do I suppose that good must therefore be insipid, sweet, weak and uninteresting? I admit that my objection to 'good' is partly my egotistical desire for me as an actress to impress; to act devious, clever, complicated and interesting. Yet surely good need not be passive. She can still be full-blooded, womanly, wise and humorous. My internal dialogues are so devious, clever, complicated and interesting that more often than not I forget where I started and can't find the way out.

I look up 'virtuous' – 'possessing, showing moral rectitude, chaste'; and 'innocent' – 'free from moral wrong, sinless'. I sincerely hope that a more complex facet as yet undiscovered will reveal itself in rehearsal. I paraphrase my four scenes down to the basic requirements of story-telling – Act I, Scene 2: 'Leontes, King of Sicilia, asks his wife Hermione to persuade their friend Polixenes of Bohemia to prolong his stay. Her success confirms Leontes' suspicion of her adultery' – and the first legible note to myself on my script is 'Think pregnant.' We 'talk' a lot.

Patrick Stewart plays Leontes. What is our relationship? We speculate about past history. We attempt to discuss the 'now' of this first scene when they are together. They are a King and a Queen. They have a son and a friend, and Hermione is well nigh nine months pregnant. Patrick Stewart, Ray Jewers who plays Polixenes, and myself are parents of children and consequently partners of parents. We exchange experiences of pregnancy. I admit to a state of introverted self-satisfaction which allowed for no intrusion and blinded me to needs outside myself, while the men acknowledge certain feelings of impotent isolation and rejection. Might this account for Hermione's apparent unawareness of Leontes' condition and her innocently provocative behaviour. If Hermione is in a state of maternity this can embrace not only the child that she has and the child that she carries but also her husband and his friend in an entirely chaste and compassionate love. This gave me a clearer understanding of her virtuousness. But discussions, though interesting, entertaining and enlightening, are easy: how 'to suit the action to the word' remains to be solved.

Hermione is not a large part. Practically, this means I have to share rehearsal time and my calls for attention are sporadic. I find this very difficult. My adrenalin is often dammed; progress is halting – one step forward and two steps back; and the time between one rehearsal and the next arid and frustrating. I am confirmed in my opinion that it is easier to play a large part. There is a limit to the degree I can progress in a solitary state. Having exposed myself to my fellow actors in an open forum, the sounds I make on my own are hollow. I go through my lines at home one night congratulating myself on my intelligent and fluid reading when a small voice from the great height of his bunk in the next room calls, 'Mummy, why are you talking in that funny voice?' I am rendered mute. I still search for that hidden clue that Hermione is not as she seems and try not to think about the orange-seller.

Following Ron Eyre's intention to be as simple as possible, Chris Dyer's model for the set presents us with a stark and awesome wall set behind a raised platform which comes to be known as 'the hotplate' where the main action will be focussed. We therefore begin to 'move' on a rehearsal floor with tape marking the area of 'the hotplate' and I wear a pregnant padding which comes in for a deal of ribald comment but which I grow quite fond of over the weeks. We improvise my playing the first scene guilty – as if Leontes has justifiable cause for suspicion – which is fun to play (very wicked and delicious), but observation on the exercise is that it is perverse and destructive to attempt to give Leontes a rational jealousy. Hermione must personify all that is pure and right in order to illuminate the irrationality of his jealousy and the extent of his loss. Polixenes says, 'This jealousy is for a precious creature, as she's rare/Must it be great.'

I attempt to play the scene aware that something is wrong – indefinable but wrong. I follow it through to my next scene, Act 2, Scene 1; Hermione is publicly accused and sent to prison. My apparent impatience and abstraction with my son Mamillius is given a very clear motivation if I am concerned about my husband. But it negates the shock of my accusation, and search as I might, and go through that scene and the next, I can find no indication that she was aware, even in retrospect, of anything that would have forewarned her of her predicament.

Therefore the first major conclusion that I adhere to is that my egotistical approach to the role is overruled and I have to accept that there is no disguise for me in this part. I cannot affect a perversity of nature, a quirk, a physical characteristic to convey psychological deviation. She is, in effect, a catalyst and the graph of her journey through the play is relatively level.

I look up 'catalysis' – 'effect produced by a substance that without undergoing change itself aids a chemical change in other bodies'. I also look up 'cipher' – 'arithmetical symbol of no value in itself but multiplying number it is placed after by ten; person or thing of no importance'. She is not a cipher! She is a woman, and I am a woman, and so I have to endow her with me and my complexities, the sum of my experience. Easier said than done. How? Courage and gall. And so my brief in the first scene is to present to the best of my ability 'a good woman'. A fundamental decision that I can move on from. And I can still 'show off' as the orange-seller.

My perennial notes for myself: not to pose like a frustrated ballet dancer, which I am. Not to talk too fast or put on that funny voice, which I do. To look up to the 'gods' when I'm thinking and not down to Hades. Avoid imitation and cliché. Be economical. Listen to the scenes I'm not in and search for clues in oblique directions. Give a thought to the time scale; time of days, time of year, time change; my relationship to other people in the play – and open myself to a sensual and tactile awareness, touch, sight, sound, scent. I attend fittings for my costumes which are pale, soft, light and lovely. I hope I have something scarlet and awe-full for my orange-seller. I have my hair cropped short for the trial scene and decide on a long blonde wig for the first scenes.

27 'What? Have I twice said well?'

And if I can conquer 'good' in the first scenes at least I'll be able to go to town in the trial scene. Act 3, Scene 2, Hermione is tried; the oracle proves her innocent, but the news of the death of her son Mamillius causes her to fall down dead. I will beat my breast, tear my hair and emit real tears. We discussed manacles – I fancy being dragged on by what is left of my hair, in chains from head to foot. But – by trial and error (excuse the pun) and an excess of courage and gall, we realize that Hermione's speech in the trial scene cannot be performed on an emotive wail (cathartic as it is to attempt as an acting exercise). The speech is too long; it becomes self-pitying, which Hermione is not.

Her speech has a fluidity and simplicity compared to the more complex intellectual agility of the first scene, where she played with words. She is articulate, objective and strong, because she is right. She is innocent and she knows it. She does not have to plead her cause or prove that she is true. She has faith. As Joan of Arc heard her voices, so does Hermione believe. To present the words as naked of imposition or comment as possible and yet to endow them with the full value of their worth is a challenge that I trust, if but partly achieved, will prove more moving, and a simple shift, bare feet and hand-cuffs will suggest all that needs to be said about her physical condition. I spend my hours discovering and caring for the nuances of meaning in Hermione's speech to the court, and the delicate balance of a stress that can illuminate or confuse. She says, 'Sir, you speak a language that I understand not. My life stands in the level of your dreams, which I'll lay down.' The complexities of that phrase have to be excavated, minutely examined and then reassembled to their original simplicity.

> For Polixenes
> (With whom I am accused), I do confess
> I loved him as in honour he required;
> With such a kind of love as might become
> A lady like me; with a love even such,
> So, and no other, as yourself commanded;
> Which not to have done I think had been in me
> Both disobedience and ingratitude
> To you and toward your friend, whose love had spoke,
> Even since it could speak, from an infant, freely,
> That it was yours. (3.2.61–71)

I tried that on my cat. Tried to make her understand the meaning of the words; tried to make it rational and colloquial and staccato, with a cup of tea in my hand and a fag in my mouth. She just went on licking her bum. But when I allowed the words to flow one into the other, to use the vowels and the syllables of each word with intent – I seduced her then – or was she just hungry? Anyway, it helped me.

But there's still the statue scene (Act 5, Scene 3) in which the statue of Hermione comes to life and she is reunited with her husband and daughter, Perdita, after sixteen years. Oh! what a chance to go to town! Even thinking about the possibility of how to express the emotions at such an event brings tears to my eyes. But – it is not reality, it is fiction. It is not a documentary drama; it is a fairy tale. And finally after many hours of tortuous experiment and emotive argument – 'the simpler the better' seems to be the answer – our discussions reach extraordinary heights of metaphysical revelation. Whether she died and was born again; whether she lived in that removed home and nightly cried herself to sleep; whether she was indeed turned to stone? If asked to comment, as I regularly am, I say, 'She stopped.' She removed herself from life until the time was ripe for her re-emergence. 'I have preserved myself', she says to Perdita – in a sort of Zen-like aspic. But I find it indefinable in mere cerebral terms. 'It is required you do awake your faith', Shakespeare asks of us. Henry Moore has said:

It is a mistake for a sculptor or a painter to speak or write very often about his job. It releases tension needed for his work. By trying to expose his aims with rounded-off, logical exactness he can easily become a theorist whose actual work is only a caged-in exposition of conceptions evolved in terms of logic and words.

I carry around with me a picture of the statue of Queen Uta in Naumburg Cathedral and have been so involved in thinking myself marble that I have almost forgotten about the orange-seller. Which is just as well, because when I finally pluck up courage to ask, it seems she was suggested as the result of a mental aberration and is now totally redundant. As is our Hymn to Apollo. Maybe we can revive them both for the end-of-season cabaret!

So I will have to make do with Hermione. We have a first run-through of the play in front of the company. I have feelings of totally selfish paranoia. Will my fellow actors think I'm good? Will I get a bigger part next season if I am? Will I ever work again? I go through my performance in a state almost amounting to schizophrenia. 'Schizophrenia' – 'a mental disease marked by disconnection between thoughts, feelings and actions'. Oh! yes. Everybody else seems to be awfully good. Geoffrey Hutchings as Autolycus makes me laugh. Robert Eddison as Antigonus makes me cry. And I can't even redeem myself as the orange-seller.

The whole company ups camp and moves to Stratford to prepare for technical and dress rehearsals. The next few days are preoccupied with the practicalities of the theatre. I am presented with an envelope of information, which tells me who is who, what is what, and where to find them, with an accompanying map which looks like Hampton Court Maze. I am also provided with a safety manual which includes such ominous paragraphs as, 'A performer's job involves a certain amount of risk so you should take all reasonable precautions to minimise those risks to ensure your own and everybody else's safety', and 'Always report any potential hazard.' I wonder whether I should warn that we have a public dress rehearsal ahead!

I am allocated a dressing-room which will become a very personal and private sanctuary. I share it with Joe Marcell, who plays Puck in *A Midsummer Night's Dream*. He leaves me little sprinklings of gold-dust in transit. I am also allocated a dresser, Maggie, for whom in the ensuing months many thanks. I regard myself in my new wig, make-up, padding and costume; and the tenuous grasp I have upon my role thus far seems to slip further away. I worry about the amount of time I have to change my costumes between scenes. I practise stepping on and off the hotplate without walking up my dress. We rehearse my being carried from the stage at the end of the trial scene. My hopes of a pathetic exit in the arms of one strong man are dashed with the humiliating realization that I am too heavy and am therefore bundled into the wings by two. I bruise my knee falling to the floor and resort to wearing knee pads under my shift. I then bruise my elbow, but draw the line at yet more padding, or I'll end up with shoulder pads and a visor like an American football player.

We rehearse bringing on the statue. I am to be discovered on a raised and curtained platform which looks something like a shower cabinet. It does not help my task to keep very still when it is suggested to me, just before I go on, that I should be revealed wearing a bath hat and singing 'I'm going to wash that man right out of my hair.' I attempt to move my concentration to more lofty sentiments and stand very very still and look very very lovely in a very very soft light and think 'Have I got enough money to pay the babysitter?', and 'I must remember to fill up the car with petrol.' Through many hours of waiting and fretting I resolve that I must be productive in this very long nightly wait that I will have between falling dead at my trial and being resurrected as a statue. I will learn Welsh, write a novel and tackle my apparently bottomless pile of overdue correspondence, and resist the gossip and giggle in the greenroom.

The tannoy in my dressing-room comes alive and there is an awful inevitability about 'Part one beginners, your call please. All those involved in the beginning of the play and masque stand by. Prop staff stand by on cue one. Musicians stand by on cue one. Stage staff stand by on cue one. Elex and sound operators stand by and Mr Jewers's dressers stand by to collect robe. Part one beginners, this is your call.'

The rehearsal space in Leicester Square has developed a sort of womb-like security and familiarity. The nakedness of the stage and the void of the auditorium now have to be given life. The transition is hard. Behind is safety – before is danger, exposure and challenge, and the audience provides us with a point of no return – a surging of adrenalin and an exchange of energy that no amount of rehearsal or theoretical anticipation can simulate. My lungs expand to fill the space, and sounds that I attempted to make in class or rehearsal are given a freedom and confidence to express themselves, and from then on it is a continuing growing and learning process. The shell, the shape and the form have been rehearsed, but the flesh and the blood are revealed in front of an audience.

In between times I giggle and gossip in the greenroom, and resolve to be more productive in my long break. The audience teaches me how to pace my performances. I am still inclined to speak too fast and therefore think too quickly and consequently not make points clear. The audience tells me where to place my performance. I observe that I have played the whole of the first scene almost entirely in profile – presuming that if I am truthful enough the audience will be able to read my ears! It is a technicality that I find hard – to show myself more generously. I admit to feelings of dissatisfaction with my ability to 'get hold of' the part. I get to turn my feet out towards the audience and dance on the top of the show, carrying myself through the first scene with a direct physical energy which from then on needs to be manufactured against the difficulty of my few scenes being disparate – there is an hour's wait between my penultimate appearance and my final one.

The first two scenes are too brief; the contact I make with other characters cursory. The trial scene has an isolated kind of challenge, while the final scene is mainly a technical exercise in how to stand still. But the audiences are enthusiastic. A number of people wait at the stage-door for my autograph and tell me how good I was in *The Duchess of Duke Street*, and my son likes the bear best. I have a salutary experience some months into the run of the play when an understudy, Peter Land, goes on for Polixenes. I find I have become dependent on a very particular habit and insidiously stuck in a comfortable groove. A new sound in the orchestra, as it were, startles me out of my inertia and to listen and respond and convey my thoughts and intentions to a fresh counterpart is very instructive.

I am asked to write an account of my approach to the role of Hermione. My initial response to the request is 'No.' I would not know where to begin and anyway it is not a part that I find very satisfying to play or indeed my playing of it an achievement with which I am satisfied. Therefore it might be interesting to attempt to analyse why. And at least it will give me something to do in my long break. So –

All those involved in the statue scene stand by please. Miss Jones, Mr Stewart, Miss Hancock, Miss Mellinger, Mr Jewers, Mr Lloyd, Mr Chelsom and all those involved in the statue scene. Props stand by and stage staff stand by to plug in the statue.

Caliban in
The Tempest
DAVID SUCHET

D AVID SUCHET is an Associate Artist of the Royal Shakespeare
Company. He joined the Company in 1973, after repertory
experience that ranged from Shylock to Reg in *The Norman Con-
quests*. He is also an experienced film and television actor, and his one-man
show, *The Kreutzer Sonata*, won him the 1979 Pye Award for Radio Actor
of the Year. At Stratford his versatility has been given scope in productions
at The Other Place and in the variety of his Shakespearean roles at the
Royal Shakespeare Theatre. In his first season of 1973, for instance, he
played Tybalt, Orlando and Tranio; in his last of 1981, he played Shylock
and Achilles. In between, he was Bolingbroke to Alan Howard's Richard
II, and Caliban to Michael Hordern's Prospero. This production of *The
Tempest*, directed by Clifford Williams, with Ralph Koltai as designer,
played in repertoire for 84 performances in 1978–9.

I had only seen one performance of *The Tempest*, and that was at
Nottingham Playhouse in about 1965. I remembered very little about the
play, although I seem to recall that Caliban was played covered in long hair.
Since that time I had become more familiar with Shakespeare – familiar
enough to know that Caliban was one of the great, although not large, parts
in the canon. Therefore when I was offered the role in 1978 I said, 'Yes,
please.' I always suspect that an actor's favourite time is between having
been offered the part and the first read-through. So it was with me.
Everyone I told that I was going to play Caliban said, 'Marvellous' or 'How
are you going to play him?', or 'Are you going to wear a special skin like a
fish and have scales and fins?' I couldn't help thinking, What do they
mean?

The first read-through went smoothly enough and because of lack of
time Clifford Williams, the director, didn't have a long talk about the play
or his own concepts. After a couple of days, though, I was called for a

28   'All the charms
Of Sycorax, toads, beetles, bats, light on you!'
David Suchet as Caliban, April 1978

meeting with him to discuss the character. I reread the play a couple of times and got a few impressions of the role – the first being that I felt rather angry that everybody in the play seemed to *use* Caliban, the second being that here was a person trying to get back something that belonged to him (his island) – something that he not only loved a great deal but something that he needed for his very existence. On meeting Clifford I told him that these were the only thoughts that I had got about the character. He told me that he didn't really have any concrete ideas, except that I might be half-fish, half-man (presumably I would wear fins) or possibly something deformed, like a thalidomide child. I left that meeting feeling rather depressed, as I didn't see any of this when I read the play – I felt confused. So at the first opportunity I decided to do some research into the history of how the role had been portrayed in the past.

I decided to go to the Shakespeare Centre (where old prompt-books are housed, as are past reviews of productions and also photographs). After making my request, I was sat in a chair in the reading room and all the reviews and photographs and notes of past RSC and other productions were put in front of me. I didn't know what to expect, so imagine my horror when I discovered that Caliban had been played as: (1) a fish, (2) a dog with one and/or two heads, (3) a lizard, (4) a monkey, (5) a snake, (6) half-ape, half-man, with fins for arms, (7) a tortoise. It was, in fact, Beerbohm Tree who played Caliban as a monkey and was praised for his agility in swinging from tree to tree! These were just a few of the extreme interpretations that I discovered when I delved into the books and reviews. I, once again, began to feel rather depressed but I did manage a smile when I read that, when Caliban had been portrayed as a tortoise, Prospero would turn him on his back when he became unruly. One overall feeling came over me – that of being totally miscast.

Early rehearsals continued and there were discussions about the scenes and the way they should go, but I found that I couldn't contribute anything at all. I felt hampered and I found myself resisting any move that Clifford urged me to make towards this monster with the fins. I didn't want to roll on my back like an animal for the 'Isle is full of noises' speech. I found myself losing confidence and becoming inhibited. I know that Clifford was trying to get me to respond to animal reactions and he was absolutely right to try and free me into finding a solution. But I knew that I was not going to solve the problem this way. Whenever I talk to drama students, or English students, I always say, 'It's in the text.' So to practise what I preached, I sat down and began really to study the text in detail. Like a detective I began to find clues which led to other clues; I was in search of a character and I was determined to find him, no matter what! I started by looking at what other characters say about Caliban. Of particular note were the following: *Miranda* – 'It is a villain, sir, I do not love to look upon'; *Trinculo* – 'A fish'; *Prospero* – 'monster', 'disproportioned', 'devil, a born devil', 'demi-devil', 'thing of darkness', 'deformed'. It was very obvious to me why Caliban had been portrayed as an evil deformed 'thing'. And then I discovered the first clue which was to send me diving into the text for more evidence. Prospero says:

> Then was this island –
> Save for the son that she did litter here,
> A freckled whelp hag-born – not honoured with
> A human shape.
>
> ARIEL   Yes, – Caliban her son –
> PROSPERO   Dull thing, I say so. He, that Caliban
> Whom now I keep in service.   (1.2.281–6)

It's obvious, I thought, why Caliban had been played as a dog or a puppy-headed monster or totally deformed. But then I discovered on further study that Prospero's speech meant something quite different. In every edition I studied, including the First Folio, there were punctuation marks or parentheses after the word 'island' and before 'not honoured'. Thus in reality Prospero's speech is saying, 'Then was this island not honoured with a human shape, save for (except for) the son that she did litter here, a freckled whelp, hag-born.' In other words, Caliban was the only one on the island with a human shape. I can remember my excitement at this discovery and continued my study with tremendous fervour. Suddenly I hit upon another quote. Miranda says that Ferdinand

> Is the third man that e'er I saw, the first
> That e'er I sighed for.   (1.2.446–7)

Who or how many men had Miranda actually seen? Well, there is her father, that's number one. Ferdinand is number three. Ariel is invisible, and Miranda hasn't met any other survivors of the shipwreck. Caliban is or can be the only other man she could have met. So far, then, my hunch was that Caliban had a human shape and was recognizable as a man, and so far the text justified this. I continued my study of the text with now a slight trepidation, and then I came across Trinculo's first speech in 2.2. Oh dear, I thought, Caliban can't be anything but a fish. My dismay grew and grew as I read and reread:

A fish, he smells like a fish . . . a strange fish . . . his fins like arms . . .

(2.2.25–34)

I paused – 'fins *like arms*'. Shakespeare did *not* write 'arms like fins'. And I started to read the speech again and it became so clear to me that Shakespeare was not describing a fish-like man but a human being whose appearance, let alone his smell, was strange to Trinculo. For the sake of this discussion I will recall the situation and textual facts. Trinculo has just been saved from drowning after a shipwreck. He has landed on a beach and comes across a 'thing' covered by gabardine. 'What have we here?', he says, 'a man or a fish? dead or alive? A fish: he smells like a fish.' There can be no doubt that Caliban has a pretty terrible smell. Then Trinculo refers to the practice in England of putting natives in fairgrounds so that people might pay money to view these monsters:

Were I in England now, as once I was, and had but this fish painted, not a holiday fool there but would give a piece of silver. There would this monster make a man. Any strange beast there makes a man. When they will not give a doit to relieve a lame beggar they will lay out ten to see a dead Indian. (2.2.27–33)

Next, Trinculo obviously looks or feels under the gabardine, for he says, 'Legged like a man, and his fins like arms' (obviously he is surprised by this as he thought that Caliban *was* a fish). 'Warm, o' my troth' (obviously Caliban is not a cold-blooded creature as fish are). And then he says, 'I do now let loose my opinion, hold it no longer, *this is no fish but an islander, that hath lately suffered by a thunderbolt.*'

At this point my excitement suddenly turned to determination. Shakespeare had obviously gone to great pains (not without tongue in cheek) to describe the popular concept of the 'native'. At this time in history England was colonizing and reports of natives as 'monsters' were coming in all the time. I tried to imagine how I would feel if I had never seen an Indian or African native. I got hold of some Leni Riefensthal photographs which gave me a good idea of what I was looking for, for there in front of me were human beings with flat noses unlike mine, very stretched ears unlike mine, and some with plates in their mouths that made their lips look totally *un*human. If I met these faces in a strange land for the first time, of course I would question whether or not I was looking at part of the human race. Hence the reaction of the first explorers and the exaggerated stories of monsters. Gonzalo echoes this when in 3.3 he says about the 'shapes':

> If in Naples
> I should report this now, would they believe me?
> If I should say I saw such islanders –
> For, certes, these are people of the island –
> Who, though they are of monstrous shape, yet note
> Their manners are more gentle-kind than of
> Our human generation you shall find. (3.3.27–33)

These textual discoveries led me to enquire whether or not Caliban ever makes reference, in the play, to his own looks. He does not. But then I thought he *must* have seen his reflection in pools of water, so why should he be afraid of Trinculo, Stephano *and* himself, or being turned into 'barnacles or . . . apes' with 'foreheads villainous low' (4.1.248–9). He has obviously seen barnacles and apes and is frightened of becoming like them. Apart from realizing from this that the monkey interpretation was for me not accurate, it was very clear that Caliban's own particular deformity was something of which he himself was unaware.

Then I decided to look at the character in terms of his physical actions. He carries logs, makes fires, builds dams for catching fish and is Prospero's slave: Prospero says he 'serves in offices that profit us'. He is also supposed to have attempted to rape Miranda. All these discoveries made it clear to me that Caliban couldn't be further away from a fish or a lizard or a puppy or a tortoise or a snake or even a monkey with fish fins. More than this, I believed that Shakespeare himself took, as I have said, great pains to give clues to this fact. 'The monster' was in the eyes of the beholder.

What became interesting with more study was the fact that Shakespeare never allows his audience to know *exactly* where this island is situated. There is Ariel's reference in 1.2 to the 'still-vexed Bermoothes' but it seems that this was a place where Ariel was sent to rather than where they were. I think it is pretty clear, though, that they were somewhere in the Mediterranean, since the wedding group set out from Italy to go to the coast of North Africa (Tunis) and on the way back were blown off course and shipwrecked. Also with further study I found out that North American Indians used to build dams to catch their fish ('No more dams I'll make for fish'). Also that the Aborigine was being used as slave labour ('Nor fetch in firing, / At requiring, / Nor scrape trenchering nor wash dish'). Also I wonder if Shakespeare knew that the Eskimo used to worship, and indeed some still do, the moon (Caliban actually believes Stephano when he says he 'was the man-i'-th'-moon' when he replies, 'I have seen thee in her. And I do adore thee'). Also that natives in this present day and age, and from time immemorial, have believed and practised black magic and sorcery. I also discovered that the word 'Calibaun' was the Romany (the gypsy) word for black. It is believed that Shakespeare was familiar with Romany. It became clear to me that Shakespeare wrote the character of Caliban as a mixture of different types of native, and showed his audience the native whose land has been taken away. This would tie in with the colonizing that was going on at the time he was writing. Shakespeare's Caliban is a basic man, a man without learning, without fine intelligence but capable of an enormous amount of uninhibited love and brutal savagery. When Prospero refers to Caliban as 'this thing of darkness' Shakespeare, I think, is punning on behaviour and/or the physical appearance. I was now clear in my own mind what I wanted to do as far as characterization was concerned. The next step was the process of discovery in the rehearsal room. When I told Clifford Williams about my findings I do believe he became as excited as I was and left me very much to my own devices in rehearsals. I was very lucky indeed that I was working with such generous and talented actors as Michael Hordern (Prospero), Richard Griffith (Trinculo) and Paul Moriarty (Stephano). They endured my pouncing on them with enormous savagery, pouting at them with affection, and at times being totally crazy.

I think it would be clearer at this point to discuss each of Caliban's scenes and to show how the interpretation became solidified. The emotional content of any character comes, and must come, with the usage of language which the playwright has given that character to utter. We use the word 'persona' when describing someone's personality or character. In Latin 'per sona' means 'through sound' (the original persona seems to have meant a mask worn by a character, and then came to mean the character himself – and one of the things a mask did was to amplify the voice in order to be heard in large open-air theatres). Shakespeare more than any other playwright I know helps the actor enormously with his characterizations, by the very words and language and verse that he gives that character. Let us take for example what Caliban says on his first entrance:

> As wicked dew as e'er my mother brushed
> With raven's feather from unwholesome fen
> Drop on you both. A south west blow on ye,
> And blister you all o'er. (1.2.321–4)

This obviously is a curse. But on further investigation the main consonants in the speech are m's, f's and b's. In other words they are mainly 'lip' consonants and therefore explode out from the mouth. If these consonants are savoured and used by the actor, it is impossible for this speech to be delivered as even politely angry. We also see a man who has very little respect (but great fear nonetheless) for his master, or his childhood playmate, Miranda. I realized also that Shakespeare, just before Caliban's entrance, has Ariel demanding his own 'liberty' and immediately Caliban demanding that his island should be given back to him.

> This island's mine, by Sycorax my mother,
> Which thou tak'st from me. (1.2.331–2)

One of the interesting things about this particular speech was that I noticed how gentle the language becomes when Caliban talks about his island – 'the fresh springs, brine pits, barren place and fertile' – the places that he showed Prospero. And then immediately aggressive with 'Curst be I that did so' and also with 'Here you *sty* me.' Caliban's language is so very pure. Pure in its gentle passages and pure in its aggressive passages. Finally, in that first scene, apart from learning that Caliban's language – i.e. English – has been taught him, we also see at the end of the scene the slave cowering under the power of his master, and he goes off to fetch fuel.

The first impression of Caliban is very important. Summarized, it is this. An angry man comes out of his cave dwelling, demanding that his island should be returned to its rightful owner and then curses the two people to whom he is talking. He then states how much he once loved them, and then in the same breath utters his lifelong regret that he ever did so. The first image therefore is one of pain and enlightenment. In this first scene we learn from Prospero that the reason Caliban has been exiled to a cave and treated harshly is because

> thou did'st seek to violate
> The honour of my child. (1.2.347–8)

Caliban's reply is ironic and very basic.

> O ho, O ho, would't had been done!
> Thou did'st prevent me, I had peopled else
> This isle with Calibans. (1.2.349–51)

But was Caliban's attempt at procreation such a sin? If, as I believe, Shakespeare wrote a native, or basic man, why should he ever feel guilty about such an attempt? Isn't survival of the species a basic instinct? Surely it is Prospero with his sophistication who translates Caliban's attempts as pure lust. In any case we know that Caliban had his education from Miranda and Prospero and I doubt very much if part of that education included the correct way to behave towards a person of the opposite sex!

The next time we see Caliban he enters carrying logs and he immediately is given to cursing Prospero. His language once again is strong and the consonants explosive:

> All the infections that the sun sucks up
> From bogs, fens, flats on Prospero fall, and make him
> By inchmeal a disease. (2.2.1–3)

Caliban then shows us his fear of Prospero's sorcery and also of animals such as apes, hedgehogs and adders. It is clear from this that Caliban has an absolute belief in black magic.

And then he meets up with two seamen, Trinculo and Stephano – 'Fine things, an if they be not sprites'. But he immediately singles out Stephano as a 'brave god' that 'bears celestial liquor – I will kneel to him.' Here we see Caliban ready, almost willingly, to make himself a slave, and when he learns from Stephano that he was 'the man-i'-th'-moon', he is willing to worship his new-found god and possible saviour. (This refers back to the Eskimo – when practising their sorcery, or when they are making curses, they hold an effigy of that person in their hand – hence the effigy I have in my hand when cursing Prospero (see Fig. 28).) We then see a mirror image of how the American Indian completely and willingly subjugated himself to the new settlers. Caliban offers Stephano everything in gentle and touching speeches:

> I'll show thee the best springs. I'll pluck thee berries.
> I'll fish for thee, and get thee wood enough. (2.2.160–1)

I then noticed the sudden change in the tone of language with his next lines,

> A plague upon the tyrant that I serve;
> I'll bear him no more sticks, but follow thee,
> Thou wondrous man.

and immediately after with

> I prithee let me bring thee where crabs grow;
> And I with my long nails will dig thee pig-nuts;
> Show thee a jay's nest, and instruct thee how
> To snare the nimble marmoset. I'll bring thee
> To clustering filberts and sometimes I'll get thee
> Young scammels from the rock. Wilt thou go with me? (2.2.167–72)

These lines may be spoken under the influence of Stephano's 'celestial liquor' but they demonstrate so beautifully Caliban's deep love for his island.

Lastly in the scene, Caliban finally rejects Prospero as his master and goes off to serve Stephano. He never really takes to Trinculo, whose comments he doesn't like. I even think that Caliban is jealous of the friendship between the two men, although there is no strong evidence in the text for this; only that Caliban definitely dislikes Trinculo.

Caliban's final song at the end of this scene I saw as a dance and song of freedom. I remember working on this at home and I must admit that it took a great deal of courage to do it in rehearsal. I beat my feet on the floor rather like a tribal dance – threw away my effigy of Prospero with 'Farewell master; farewell, farewell.' And then sang very loudly the song 'No more dams I'll make for fish', etc., and when I got to 'Freedom, high-day, high-day freedom, freedom high-day, freedom!', I stopped singing but let those words come out of my body as though released from the depths of my soul; sometimes the words would literally lift me off the floor. And in this state of wild exuberance the scene closed with Caliban having found a new god and a new hope. The next time we see Caliban he is still in the company of Trinculo and Stephano and all three are a little more than drunk, as

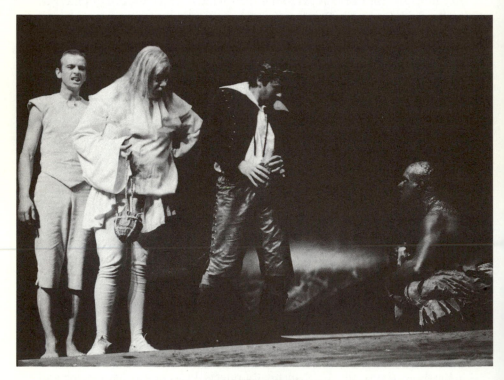

29 'Thou liest'
Caliban with Ariel (Ian Charleson), Stephano (Richard Griffith) and Trinculo (Paul Moriarty)

Stephano has ordered that only 'When the butt is out, we will drink water, not a drop before.' It is now that we see in front of us the real dislike that Caliban has of Trinculo because he 'mocks me'. He even asks Stephano to 'Bite him to death, I prithee.' What I noticed in this scene was something that became a vital part of my characterization. It was a point of language. I noticed that, excepting the early part of the scene, which is in prose, when Caliban begins to speak in verse it is about Prospero. His language is bitter, ugly and extremely aggressive when he asks Stephano to

> brain him
> Having first seized his books. Or with a log
> Batter his skull, or paunch him with a stake,
> Or cut his wesand with thy knife.   (3.2.88–91)

He then says

> Remember
> First to possess his books; for without them
> He's but a sot as I am.   (3.2.91–3)

How amazing, I thought, that here is a man that knows he is unintelligent but doesn't care. A man who accepts what he is and obviously despises the type of person that is the outcome of 'learning' which is personified, for Caliban, by Prospero. Also, only thirty lines later do we see the complete antithesis of this aggression when Caliban tells Stephano

> Be not afeared, the isle is full of noises,
> Sounds, and sweet airs, that give delight and hurt not.
> Sometimes a thousand twangling instruments
> Will hum about mine ears; and sometimes voices,
> That if I then had waked after long sleep,
> Will make me sleep again; and then in dreaming,
> The clouds methought would open, and show riches
> Ready to drop upon me, that when I waked
> I cried to dream again.   (3.2.135–43)

And then only two lines later when he perceives that Stephano is coming round with 'This will prove a brave kingdom to me where I shall have my music for nothing', Caliban spits out, 'When Prospero is destroyed.'

What basic, raw extremes of emotion – from *hate* (about Prospero) to *love* (about his island) to *hate* (about Prospero) – are encountered in so brief a spell. It was at this discovery that I realized that Caliban's thoughts and actions are as totally instinctive as is his language, and not coloured by intelligence but by his gut feelings. This discovery led to my playing a Caliban at times dangerous and at times childish, but at all times totally spontaneous. The other thing about the 'isle is full of noises' speech is that he is totally in touch with and part of *nature* even though he may have no understanding of what nature is. It shows complete trust and faith in his home and is the most important possession that he has – indeed his island is really the only thing he has.

From this point on in the play, Caliban's story starts to go wrong. It is as though Shakespeare, although showing us Caliban's plight, is also trying to show us that premeditated or indeed any murder is no answer and is basically an evil deed. Shakespeare couldn't really allow Caliban to win; and it is in the next scene that we see the results of this premeditation. The thought of usurping Prospero, with the fact that Caliban has been treating Stephano like a god, has gone to Stephano's head; but with macabre humour both Trinculo and Stephano are lured from the murder by fine clothes. Caliban's frustration is at its height when he tells them

> We shall lose our time,
> And all be turned to barnacles, or to apes
> With foreheads villainous low.   (4.1.247–9)

The scene ends with all three of them being chased by Prospero's dogs and hounds. They have been caught. In the last scene the murderous plot is uncovered and Prospero orders Caliban to

> Go, sirrah, to my cell,
> Take with you your companions. As you look
> To have my pardon, trim it handsomely.   (5.1.292–4)

Caliban's reply can really only be one of submission, as he is in fear of being pinched to death:

> Ay, that I will. And I'll be wise hereafter,
> And seek for grace. What a thrice double ass
> Was I to take this drunkard for a god,
> And worship this dull fool.   (5.1.295–8)

It is obvious from this speech that Caliban has learned by his experience. I did, however, decide that the first line and a half of this last speech should be tinged with slight irony. I think that Caliban has learned that being obedient he will be safe. But when anybody else should ever come to his island again he certainly won't even try to befriend them – he will kill on sight.

Having now worked through the whole play and decided how the scenes should be played, I then worked out with the designer, Ralph Koltai, and the head of the make-up department, Brenda Leedham, what I should wear and how I should look. I remember in rehearsals there was a discussion about the possibility of being totally naked but I dismissed this immediately! After all, how could Prospero allow me to be naked after having tried to violate his daughter? Maybe before that event occurred but certainly not afterwards. Then Ralph had a very good idea – why not wear one of Prospero's cast-offs? He designed a pair of breeches with slits in them; they were a dirty fawn colour and came to below my knees; apart from this I was bare-chested and barefoot. Then Brenda designed a most ingenious make-up. I wanted to look like 'basic man' and I wanted to be of a blackish hue. But I didn't want to be instantly recognizable as being obviously an African native or an Indian or an Eskimo or an Aborigine. I wanted to look like the quintessential native and Brenda with her extraordinary talents made two rubber prosthetics which covered my eyebrows and gave me a prehistoric-looking forehead. Then she made me an African nose but we decided against frizzy, tightly matted hair and instead she made the top of my head appear bald and lumpy by placing dollops of porridge on it and covering the whole top of my head with latex. The result was unbelievably effective. Then I put on two layers of dark brown make-up all over my body and then sprayed it pewter-coloured. Under the stage lighting the effect was that sometimes I would look black, sometimes pewter, and sometimes I even took on a greenish hue.

The voice I used was slightly stilted as I tried to make it clear that I had been taught to speak and my physical movements were very slightly ape-like without *being* an ape. For example, I would be slightly crouched and bent forward with my movement, and I would squat rather than sit. I must say that, as far as Caliban's language having been taught him and, as he puts it, 'my profit on't / Is, I know how to curse', I find it ironic that some of the finest poetry in the play should come out of the mouth of this self-recognized 'sot'. With this fact in mind I wonder whose side Shakespeare was really on, Prospero's or Caliban's? And also whether Shakespeare ever really intended Caliban to be a fish or a man? I know what I think.